HOMESTEAD DECLARATIONS

AMENDED INDEX

Sonoma
County
California

—Second Edition—

Sonoma County
Genealogical Society

HERITAGE BOOKS
2011

HERITAGE BOOKS
AN IMPRINT OF HERITAGE BOOKS, INC.

Books, CDs, and more—Worldwide

For our listing of thousands of titles see our website
at
www.HeritageBooks.com

Published 2011 by
HERITAGE BOOKS, INC.
Publishing Division
100 Railroad Ave. #104
Westminster, Maryland 21157

International Standard Book Numbers
Paperbound: 978-0-7884-5313-7
Clothbound: 978-0-7884-8747-7

Introduction

This is the second edition of *Amended Index, Sonoma County Homestead Declarations*, the first edition having been printed in 1985 under the direction of Eugenia Titus Ohman, Projects Chair of the Sonoma County Genealogical Society at that time.

The purpose of the Homestead Act, signed by President Lincoln on May 20, 1862, was to encourage settlement in the western states on unappropriated public land. Any person who was 21 years old, or head of a family, or met certain military requirements was eligible to apply for a homestead. Three steps were required: (1) file an application, (2) improve the land, and (3) file for deed of title. Any person who had borne arms against the U.S., or given aid and comfort to its enemies, was not eligible. This was a significant point since the Homestead Act was passed during the early years of the Civil War.

The maximum amount of land that could be entered (moved onto) was 160 acres, or one-quarter section. The homesteader had to live on the land continuously and cultivate it for a period of five years in order to obtain the patent.

In Sonoma County, the patents are available on microfilm in the Office of the Sonoma County Recorder. The first recorded declaration in Sonoma County was made 5 June 1860 (some declarations were made before passage of the statute). The patents read much like any deed, and basic information was abstracted by volunteers of the Sonoma County Genealogical Society. When family information (marital status, relationship) was included in the patent, it was also abstracted and included along with the name of the applicant.

Abbreviations Used

w/o	without
yrs.	years
dec'd	deceased
aka	also known as
est.	estate
inc.	includes
mo(s).	month(s)

Women's Names found in Sonoma County Homestead Declarations

In some cases, what was apparently the maiden name of a woman was found in the homestead application. A summary of those instances is given in this table.

Surname of Applicant	Name Shown in Declaration
Provines	Bissell, Cornelia
Commary	Burleson, Julia A.
Ford	Campbell, Mary
Reid	Cobb, Sarah
Lane	Cronin, Delia
Brockman	Culbertson, Jane
Simpson	Dalzell, Margaret A.
Walker	Ensign, Myrtle
Young	Farr, Loula
Roe	Fink, Teresa
Todd	Fiske, Alice
Granice	Hale, Grace
Jones	Hansen, Louisa
Hennessey	Harrison, Johana
Stump	Haub, Minnie S.
Clark	Hill, Antoinette
Forrester	Hooper, C. C.
Larsen	Johnson, Caroline
Fernald	Johnson, Mary Lillian
Bittman	Johnstone, Adda

White	Lewis, Edith
Palmer	Mardis, Martha A.
Ross	Mehegan, Elizabeth
Carrillo	Meyer, Elizabeth
Beatty	Milliari, Margaret A.
Grant	McCappin, Lavina
Stuart	McGaughy, Anabel
Turner	McLeod, Florence
Coon	Norris, Hannah A.
Taylor	O'Brien, Catherine
Carriger	O'Brien, Kate
Wilkins	Peterson, Emily C.
Corria	Robbins, Heter
Warren	Ryall, Maude
Richardson	Sands, Gertrude
Wiedersham	Schwitzer, Louisa
Johnson	Skaane, Karen J.
Spaulding	Trice, Maude
Ramoni	Walker, Cora
West	Werner, Augusta
Campbell	Wyman, Bessie

Acknowledgments
Eugenia Titus Ohman, Original Projects Chairman
Lois Nimmo, Data Entry, 2nd edition
Doris Dickenson, editor, 2nd edition
Carmen Finley, camera ready copy, 2nd edition

Applicant and Family Information	Filing Date	Vol.-Pg.
Abbott, G. Frank; Maude G. (L-477); 2 minor children	20 Nov. 1917	L-385
Abeel, D. K.; Jane Amelia; 2 minor children; (A-392)	10 Jan. 1906	J-118
Abell, Franklin; Emily	4 Jan. 1862	A-392
Abraham, Louis F.; Frances E.; minor children	25 May 1909	K-229
Abraio, Antonio S.; Mary; 7 children	29 Jan. 1912	K-412
Abshire, Myrtle L.; Alfred C.	16 Nov. 1895	H-318
Acker, Jane; R. W.	18 Sep. 1886	F-310
Ackerman, A. A.; O. B.	2 Jun. 1894	H-52
Ackerman, Amelia; Byron A. Ackerman	9 Jan. 1913	K-482
Ackerman, Elizabeth, wife of John D.	11 Sep. 1871	B-557
Ackerman, Mary, married	8 Jun. 1866	B-17
Ackley, E. N. & wife	11 Jul. 1877	C-570
Acors, Jacob & wife	30 Jul. 1877	C-584
Adams, Harriet Anna; Joseph & children	10 Mar. 1916	L-261
Adams, Hiram & wife	14 Jun. 1880	E-17
Adams, Mrs. Florence; Riley C. (K-385)	14 Aug. 1905	J-104
Adams, Nellie; Anias	25 Mar. 1910	K-306
Adamson, James & wife	4 Apr. 1879	D-394
Adamson, M. J., Mrs.; E. H., husband	17 Dec. 1878	D-366
Adel, Annette; Frank	25 Nov. 1884	E-522
Adler, Lewis & Martha [F-444, 13 July 1896, probate (Lewis) w/o issue]	22 Jun. 1875	C-413
Adler, Lewis; Ann	9 Feb. 1863	A-541
Agnew, Samuel J.; Emma T. (?)	1 Jun. 1866	B-15
Ahlers, Hannah; Henry	11 Sep. 1911	K-389
Ahlf, Sophie; John D.	7 Dec. 1905	J-111
Aitken, James; widower	30 Aug. 1897	H-625
Aitken, W. H. J. & wife	16 Jun. 1894	H-59
Akers, Grace M.; Stephen (J-139)	30 Jan. 1906	J-121
Akers, Stephen & wife	6 Jun. 1860	A-1
Alban, Wm. G.; Martha A.	27 Mar. 1861	A-176
Albertson, Joseph; Martha (A-617 & B-397)	25 Mar. 1861	A-179
Albright, Kate; Henry	5 Oct. 1892	G-360
Alexander, Achsah H.; Charles	17 Feb. 1885	F-23
Alexander, Mary; John	30 Jun. 1884	E-478
Allegrini, Jennie; Francis; Louie	9 Aug. 1909	K-248
Allen, B. B., widower	12 Dec. 1887	F-436
Allen, Carrie; J. K.	21 Nov. 1898	I-147

Applicant and Family Information	Filing Date	Vol.-Pg.
Allen, Henry; Laura E.	15 Nov. 1872	D-12
Allen, James J.; Mary A.	10 Jan. 1903	I-427
Allen, John W.; Leona J.	23 Aug. 1907	K-69
Allen, John; Caroline D.	25 Apr. 1861	A-310
Allen, O. S. & wife	1 Jun. 1878	D-264
Allen, Otis, married	2 Jan. 1867	B-66
Allen, William P.	22 Dec. 1874	C-360
Alley, John M.; Martha A.	21 Jun. 1870	B-423
Alley, Thos. J.; son, Charles W. Alley, 9 yrs. (mother, Sarah, C-2111)	21 Jun. 1870	B-425
Alten, Martha; Wendell	11 Apr. 1881	F-1
Alves, Helen J.; John J.	11 Jul. 1914	L-90
Ambrose, Marguerette V., widow	14 Nov. 1911	K-401
Amerman, Henry J. & wife	3 Aug. 1881	E-124
Amerman, Nella J., wife	13 Nov. 1879	D-484
Ames, Chas. G.; family	3 Jan. 1877	D-69
Ames, Mary M. C.; husband	24 Aug. 1882	E-256
Ames, Mrs. C. G.; C. G.	11 Mar. 1896	H-390
Amesbury, Wm.; wife	25 Jun. 1892	G-321
Amos, Charlotte C.; Robert. C., dec'd.	5 Dec. 1896	H-509
Anderson, A.; wife	28 Jul. 1893	G-441
Anderson, Anna M.	14 Aug. 1905	J-93
Anderson, Effa; J. J.	10 Aug. 1917	L-362
Anderson, H. Clay; Ann Frances	2 Jul. 1866	B-22
Anderson, Herbert A.; wife; 1 daughter	27 Jun. 1907	K-55
Anderson, John; wife	8 Jun. 1895	H-229
Anderson, L. S.; wife	3 Oct. 1878	D-337
Anderson, Louisa Ann; Charles	20 Mar. 1889	F-538
Anderson, Mamie; husband, Hans	9 Jan. 1917	L-325
Anderson, Maria Jepsen	27 Jun. 1917	L-357
Anderson, Wm. L.; Emma R.; (C-451)	6 Mar. 1861	A-148
Andresen, Margaretha; A. J. F.	28 Mar. 1896	H-396
Andrews, Amelia Carbline, married	16 Aug. 1875	C-431
Andrews, Eliz. J., single; (L-118)	21 Feb. 1911	K-366
Andrews, Ellen; John	19 Nov. 1917	L-383
Andrews, Mary; Robert	17 Feb. 1897	I-51
Andrews, Mrs. E. J.	17 Mar. 1903	I-437
Annis, Wm. O.; Elizabeth Ann	28 Jan. 1878	D-210

Applicant and Family Information	Filing Date	Vol.-Pg.
Applebaum, I.; Sarah; children: Samuel, 17; Jeannette, 15; Benjamin, 13	15 Dec. 1913	L-47
Appleton, Horatio; wife; 2 children	5 Jul. 1877	C-566
Arbuckle, Frances; James H.	4 Sept. 1885	F-123
Arbuckle, James H.; wife	11 Jul. 1881	E-111
Archambeau, Matilda	8 Jul. 1875	C-416
Archer, Anna C., widow; LeRoy E., minor children; (K-220)	8 Mar. 1895	H-182
Archer, Ella M.; Warren O.; & children	22 Sep. 1917	L-371
Arey, Ellen; Thomas	10 Jan. 1903	I-331
Arfsten, (Arfstein) Esther & L.	21 Apr. 1909	K-224
Armstrong, Geo.; Hettie	17 Oct. 1910	K-339
Armstrong, James; wife	3 Jun. 1901	I-333
Armstrong, Mary; husband, S. G. F.	13 Nov. 1919	M-12
Armstrong, Winifred; David	9 Feb. 1878	D-220
Arnold, Edward; wife	21 Aug. 1890	G-92
Arnold, Wm. J., married	3 Sep. 1870	B-444
Asbil, Kate; Pierce	30 Apr. 1890	G-36
Ash, Mary E.; husband, Emerson F.	7 Mar. 1916	L-257
Asti, Mrs. Julia; husband, Joseph	7 Sep. 1910	K-334
Ataido, Fastino de Souss; wife	9 Nov. 1889	F-628
Atchison, Ora M.; husband, Austin J.	12 Nov. 1914	L-115
Atchley, Geo. W., married	18 Nov. 1874	C-344
Atkins, Venia; (see Owen)	19 Aug. 1913	L-26
Atkinson, Malissa; husband, Lemuel	6 Jan. 1910	K-286
Atwood, Geo. (deceased); wife Etta; child, Ethel, a minor	29 Oct. 1906	K-11
Auser, E. W., married	30 Apr. 1868	B-233
Austin, Amos, married	6 Dec. 1870	B-472
Austin, Essie E.; husband, J. S.	22 Aug. 1906	J-148
Austin, John; Mary Agnes	26 Sep. 1893	G-470
Austin, Lillie B.; Granville T.	9 Aug. 1899	I-214
Austin, Mary E.; Granville, T.	8 Sep. 1885	F-127
Austin, Rosie; Charles; (Rose & family, 9 July 1895, F-285)	16 Nov. 1887	F-430
Avela, Flora J.; Joseph S.; Joseph, 4; Leona, 2 yrs.; (K-215)	19 Jun. 1899	I-209
Avilla, Mary J.; husband, John Maria Avilla	17 Dec. 1906	K-25
Ayers, Alexander; Elizabeth A.	28 Oct. 1864	A-621
Ayers, Martha Evelyn; husband, Clarence L.	4 Jan. 1916	L-248
Ayers, Matilda E.; husband, Charles R.; 1 child	5 Feb. 1915	L-143
Ayers, Wm., Sr.; Amelia	18 Apr. 1861	A-289

Applicant and Family Information	Filing Date	Vol.-Pg.
Babcock, Harriet; husband, M. D.	8 Jan. 1867	B-61
Babcock, Hattie R.; John H.; (F-110)	19 Dec. 1881	E-171
Babcock, Sarah F.; husband, Alfred B. F. Babcook; 3 children; (E-466; M-8)	28 Sep. 1910	K-337
Baber. James A.; wife, Luch C.	18 Apr. 1914	L-77
Baber. Randall G.; family	1 Oct. 1866	B-48
Bacci, Eva; , Alcide	13 Jan. 1910	K-287
Bacon, John S.; wife, Lucy C.	8 Mar. 1887	F-374
Bacon, Josiah	21 Mar. 1864	A-597
Bacon, L. Maude; husband, Arthur D.; Ronald I., a minor	24 Aug. 1907	K-71
Badger, Geo. W., married	23 Feb. 1878	D-223
Baer, Sarah A.; husband, George E.	4 Jun. 1906	J-135
Bagley, Ellen Antoinette; husband, I. W.	25 Dec. 1860	A-90
Bagley, Mrs. E. A.; John D.	7 Nov. 1881	E-157
Bahen, Michael; 2 minor children	5 Jan. 1884	E-415
Bahrs, Herman; wife, Only	19 Aug. 1809	I=106
Bailey, James B., married	6 Aug. 1870	b-439
Bailey, M. C.; wife	9 Aug. 1879	D-448
Bailhache, Josephine; husband, J. N.	11 Jun. 1880	D-582
Bailiff, John; wife	27 Oct. 1879	D-479
Baines, Wm. E., head of house: father, John; mother, Sarah	18 May 1898	I-75
Baker, Annie D.; husband, Albert F.; minor children; (K-309)	25 Sep. 1905	J-98
Baker, E. T., widow, Isaac dec'd.	19 Nov. 1866	B-70
Baker, Henry; wife; 3 children; (G-248)	22 Apr. 1878	C-599
Baker, Mrs. Clara, single woman; 2 sons: Wm. M., 24; Elmer, 11; probate; (I-360)	6 Jun. 1896	B-438
Baker, William, married	10 Apr. 1874	C-306
Baker, Wm. & Elmer; Clara dec'd	23 Mar. 1903	H-752
Baker, Wm.; Dorothy	1 Jul. 1864	A-511
Bale, Francisca; Edward	11 Apr. 1888	F-461
Ball, John W.; Eliza M.	17 Apr. 1861	A-233
Ballard, Emma U.; husband, Ben F.	16 Apr. 1919	L-469
Ballard, Rachel; John H.	12 Mar. 1895	H-189
Balletta, P.; wife	21 Sep. 1888	F-507
Balloti, Asunta; husband, Atillio	12 Jul. 1920	M-43
Ballow, Isaac A., married	20 May 1875	C-401
Baltz, Chas. & Anna	19 Dec. 1878	D-368
Banchieri, Achille; wife; 3 minor children	8 Aug. 1911	K-386
Banducci, Guiseppina; husband, Angelo	9 Jun. 1917	L-353

Applicant and Family Information	Filing Date	Vol.-Pg.
Bane, David A.	24 Mar. 1920	M-24
Banes, H. L.; wife, Fredricka	3 Jan. 1911	K-356
Banfield, Martha B.; husband, Fred H.	1 Dec. 1920	M-63
Bannister, Madeline; husband, Charles O.	13 Oct. 1917	L-375
Bannon, Mary; John	4 Feb. 1884	E-431
Baptista, Anselmo S.	5 Aug. 1905	J-90
Baptista, Mary; Manuel Silva	9 May 1898	I-69
Barba, Manuel; wife; 11 children	25 Aug. 1900	I-286
Barbee, Robt. J.; wife, Harriet E.	8 Aug. 1905	J-91
Barber, Dorothy C.; husband, Lewis R.	26 Aug. 1915	L-210
Barbieri, Agostino; wife, Giuiditta C.; 5 children; (K-438)	12 Apr. 1911	K-374
Barenchi, Emilia; husband, Charles, dec'd.	28 Sep. 1908	K-171
Bargagliotti, Caterina; husband, Victor	8 Mar. 1907	K-34
Barham, Helen; W. W.	31 Aug. 1903	I-465
Barham, Luda V.; Ed. C.	28 Oct. 1904	J-41
Barker, Mary Ann; C. W.	21 Apr. 1900	I-270
Barnard, Fred A.; wife, Millie F.	29 Jul.. 1913	L-17
Barnes, Alexander; Sarah	14 Dec. 1860	A-92
Barnes, Alice; Benjamin F.	3 Oct. 1898	I-127
Barnes, Eliz. A.; Wm. P.	21 May 1897	H-591
Barnes, Franklin; Seren	4 Nov. 1870	B-462
Barnes, Helena, married	6 Feb. 1875	C-368
Barnes, Henry S.; insolvent debtor; probate	23 Mar. 1896	F-4004
Barnes, J. K.; wife	24 Mar. 1882	E-198
Barnes, Ross A.; wife, Ellen	2 Sep. 1914	L-98
Barnes, Sarah F.; W. H.	27 Aug. 1896	H-476
Barnes, Thos. L., widower	15 Dec. 1860	A-85
Barnes, Velma C.; husband, Benjamin H.	9 Jan. 1920	M-17
Barnes, William P., unmarried	24 Apr. 1861	A-325
Barney, M. W. & wife	16 Nov. 1869	B-367
Barnhardt, C. M.	4 May 1897	H-586
Barrelli, Joseph; Johanna	12 Aug. 1887	F-402
Barrett, Nora L.; husband, Francis E.	4 Sep. 1909	K-256
Barricks, Catherine E.; Louis Henry	19 Oct. 1904	J-40
Barry, John; wife	18 Apr. 1862	A-441
Barry, John; Nancy L.	8 Mar. 1867	B-91
Barry, Mary, widow of Edward	18 Nov. 1882	E-287
Barth, Adam; wife, Catherine	3 Feb. 1870	B-377

Applicant and Family Information	Filing Date	Vol.-Pg.
Barth, Adam; wife, Catherine & children	14 Feb. 1876	C-493
Barth, Catherine, married	14 Jun. 1870	B-417
Bartholomew, James H. S.; wife, Helen S.; son Sherman B.; (L-50)	21 Mar. 1913	K-493
Barton, John; wife, Elizabeth A.	10 Apr. 1914	L-73
Bartsch, Anna; husband, Charles	13 Mar. 1911	K-368
Baruch, H.; Sara	16 Mar. 1861	A-155
Basso, M. Laura; husband, Ferdinand Lodo	10 Apr. 1915	L-160
Bassoni, Louis; Ella	5 Dec. 1884	E-527
Bastable, Julia; husband, B. Bastable; 3 minor children	1 Feb. 1909	K-202
Batchelder, M. L., Mrs.	6 Jan. 1877	D-74
Batchelor, Mrs. Selma; husband, John S.	6 Oct. 1910	K-338
Batchelor, Susie, unmarried; 2 minors: Wayne, 18; Elmer, 8; (J-73)	13 Mar. 1911	K-370
Batchelor, Susie, head of family; Elmer, 12 yrs.; (30 Sep. 1918, L-431)	10 Dec. 1914	L-123
Bates, Mary M.; John L.	6 Apr. 1889	F-550
Bates, Pauline; husband, W. F.	21 Mar. 1870	B-385
Bates, Phillip; Malinda M., ;B-551)	1 Apr. 1861	A-192
Bauer, Lena; Joseph	23 Oct. 1894	G-506
Bauer, Louis; wife, Sophie	26 Apr. 1861	A-350
Baum, Bridget; husband, August; probate	7 Jul. 1891	E-193
Baumeister, Rosa; husband; 3 children	6 Jun. 1905	J-75
Baur, John; wife	13 Feb. 1879	D-384
Bayler, John; wife	25 Jun. 1881	E-105
Baylis, Honorah; husband, Thomas F.	10 Nov. 1871	B-576
Beacom, Mary; Thomas; (E-130)	24 Jul. 1880	D-597
Beam, Jeremiah, married	14 May 1874	B-643
Beam, Laura P.; husband, Eben D.	24 Nov. 1914	L-117
Bean, Michael; wife, Mary	30 May 1878	D-260
Beatty, John C.; wife	29 Jul. 1876	D-34
Beatty, W. F.; wife, Margaret A. Milliari	3 Dec. 1867	B-171
Beauchamp, Eliz. A.; husband, J. O.	8 Jun. 1909	K-234
Beaujot, Felicien	19 Mar. 1920	L-22
Beaver, Mary Jane; Henry; (14 Dec. 1897, probate, G-58)	26 Feb. 1883	E-316
Becker, Mary; John	17 Mar. 1900	I-258
Beckner, Wm. D.; wife, Angeline	4 Apr. 1872	C-71
Beebe, Mary; Elijah	20 Mar. 1900	I-260
Beedle, Charlotte; Louis	12 May 1896	H-413

Applicant and Family Information	Filing Date	Vol.-Pg.
Beedle, L.; wife; (N. on notarization)	26 Jan. 1885	E-547
Beel, Annie C., widow	10 Oct. 1870	B-457
Beene, L.; wife	28 Jan. 1885	E-548
Beeson, Caroline W.; W. S.	21 Apr. 1884	E-461
Beeson, Emma; E. J.	15 Jan. 1896	H-361
Beeson, I. R.; wife	9 Apr. 1886	F-247
Beggerow, Hermann C. A.; wife, Hedwig; 2 minor children	26 Jan. 1914	L-56
Behmer, Ida A.; Daniel	12 Oct. 1897	I-1
Behmer, Ida; Daniel	13 Mar. 1899	I-192
Behmer, Mary E.; John	3 Oct. 1899	I-219
Behmer, Mary; not now married; one son; one daughter	11 Feb. 1915	L-142
Behmer, Rosa A.; John	7 Dec. 1887	F-435
Behnisch, Augusta	7 Aug. 1902	I-411
Belden, Jessie M.; husband, George M.	1 Sep. 1915	L-211
Belknap, D.; wife, & grandchild	3 Oct. 1885	F-142
Bell, Geo. S.; wife, Amelia A.; 3 children	5 Dec. 1916	L-318
Bell, J. S.; L. A., Mrs.	21 Aug. 1890	G-96
Bell, John W.; Candis A.	2 Jan. 1873	B-618
Bell, Lucy, Mrs.	5 Mar. 1878	D-228
Bell, Luther; wife	23 Sep. 1896	H-487
Bella, Victoria; children: Joseph, 8; Louise, 4 yrs.	10 Apr. 1905	J-60
Bellandi, Elvira; husband, J.	10 Jun. 1919	L-479
Bellaria, Pietra; wife, Rosa	26 Jul. 1919	L-486
Benjamin, A. M., married; (B-620)	15 Apr. 1861	A-293
Benjamin, A. M.; Lucy J.	7 Jul. 1882	E-240
Benjamin, Lucy J.; widow of A. J.; no minor children	3 Jan. 1911	K-357
Bennett, C. E.; Ada L.; no children	14 Apr. 1908	K-117
Bennett, Clarressa, unmarried	29 Dec. 1879	D-498
Bennett, Rose E.; husband, Isaac N.	3 May 1913	K-502
Bennett, Susan, married	25 Jun. 1866	B-20
Benning, Katie; Anton	24 Jul. 1900	I-280
Benson, Mary L.; husband, Henry; his son, H. Urban; her sons, Ray/Jesse	30 Mar. 1907	K-38
Berdrow, O. L.; wife	19 Dec. 1890	G-150
Berg, August, married	9 Feb. 1877	D-82
Berger, Moses; family	22 Jul. 1865	A-663
Berka, John; wife	14 Sep. 1878	D-324
Berka. F.; wife	26 Jan. 1900	I-241

Applicant and Family Information	Filing Date	Vol.-Pg.
Bernard, Lyde H.; husband, John; (M-65)	28 Nov. 1917	L-386
Berry, Allice; head of household	13 Mar. 1869	B-332
Berry, D. T.; wife, Alice	13 Oct. 1865	A-678
Berry, John; wife, Teresa E.	16 Sep. 1919	M-1
Berry, Lillie; husband, Jos. P.	28 Oct. 1907	K-81
Bertoli, Paul; wife	13 Sep. 1884	E-510
Bertoni, P.; wife, Giovanna; 5 children	20 Jun. 1914	L-86
Bethel, Chester, married	24 Apr. 1877	D-120
Bettencourt, Frank; wife, Leah	8 Feb. 1921	M-73
Beusan, John J.; wife, Mary J.	12 Oct. 1910	K-346
Bew, Caroline; husband, George; son, George H.; daughter, Jennie Prindle; probate	10 Feb. 1894	F-65
Beyer, Ernest C.; wife	5 Aug. 1893	G-445
Beyer, Ernest C.; insolvent partner, Rice & Beyer	24 Dec. 1894	H-127
Bianchini, Mary, Mrs., widow	4 Oct. 1919	M-5
Bianchini, Misaele; wife, Joseppina	7 Apr. 1914	L-71
Bice, Cornelius; Mary J.	6 Jun. 1861	A-368
Biddle, B. R.; wife	15 May 1882	E-218
Biddle, E. W.; wife	18 May 1898	I-74
Bigelow, Rosilla M.; Zadoc M.	25 Sep. 1893	G-467
Bigham, Emma; husband, Mitchel	27 Nov. 1908	K-186
Bigsby, Chas. B.; wife, Eliza	14 Mar. 1861	A-160
Bigsby, Mary J.; Milton S.	13 Jan. 1902	I-372
Billings, Eliza Ann; John F.	22 Aug. 1884	E-500
Birck, Alexander; wife, Emmaline; child 14 yrs.	6 Jul. 1908	K-141
Birck, Emmaline; husband, Alexander	28 Feb. 1908	K-104
Bird, Grace H.; Albert R.	4 Jan. 1904	I-489
Bishop, Martha; John J.	2 Nov. 1885	F-155
Bishop, T. C., dec'd.; Mary	10 Mar. 1890	G-24
Bither, Sarah Jane; M. G.	20 Jan. 1898	I-43
Bittman, Adda Johnstone; husband, L. R.; Bittmann; Mary Florence, 5 yrs.	21 Dec. 1911	K-406
Bizzini, Katie; Julius, dec'd.; no children; probate	30 Aug. 1897	G-4
Black, Ellen; Alexander	12 Mar. 1880	D-538
Black, Sarah Alice; George Henry	6 Sep. 1900	I-289
Blackburn, Allen H.; wife	27 Jan. 1899	I-173
Blackburn, Charles; wife	8 Feb. 1882	E-190
Blackburn, Charles; family	31 Jan. 1866	A-691
Blackburn, Chas.; Jemima Jane	18 Dec. 1861	A-387

Applicant and Family Information	Filing Date	Vol.-Pg.
Blackburn, Frank L.; wife, Caroline W.; (K-163)	15 May 1905	J-71
Blackburn, Jemima J.; Charles, dec'd.; probate	19 Jan. 1898	C-80
Blackburn, Maud; husband, C. W.	2 May 1913	K-501
Blair, Adel; husband, John N.	26 Sep. 1912	K-453
Blair, John; Frederike	6 Feb. 1895	H-165
Blakeley, Samuel; wife, Elizabeth	10 Apr. 1861	A-209
Blanchard, D. H.; wife, Martha A.; 1 child	16 Apr. 1908	K-118
Blanchard, Martha A.; husband, David H.	25 Jul. 1906	J-143
Blasi, Rudolph, single	23 Jun. 1898	I-90
Bledsoe, A. C.; Elizabeth D.; (B-336)	3 Feb. 1868	B-193
Blinn, Mortimer; Amanda M.	7 Oct. 1865	A-674
Bliss, E. Louise, widow of Wm. D.	23 Feb. 1887	F-360
Blosser, Thomas G.; wife, Mary J.	3 Jun. 1913	L-4
Blunden, Edna B.; husband, James	31 May 1912	K-426
Bly, Ella L.; Albert R.	31 Jul. 1899	I-212
Board, Izora O.; Wm.	27 Sep. 1901	I-357
Bobell, John C. A.; wife, Emma; no children	25 May 1908	K-127
Bocca, Angelina; Francisco	7 Nov. 1900	I-302
Bock, David; Lucy	20 Apr. 1861	A-274
Boehm, Oscar; Wilhelmina	27 May 1898	I-78
Boehm, Wilhelmina; Oscar	31 May 1898	I-82
Boesch, Jacob; wife, Bertha	12 Aug. 1908	K-152
Boggess, Minnie, Mrs.; husband, R. G.	21 Aug. 1917	L-364
Boggiano, Domenico; wife	22 Dec. 1900	I-309
Boggs, Fred C. S., married	24 Oct. 1876	D-39
Boggs, Geo. W., married,; (C-43)	19 Jan. 1878	D-201
Boggs, Joseph O.; Deborah A.; (C-154)	13 May 1874	B-642
Boggs, William M.; wife, Sonora	24 Apr. 1862	A-468
Bohnenberger, Luella D.; Chas. U.	18 Sep. 1899	I-217
Boido, Erminia; husband, Guiseppe	4 Dec. 1907	K-83
Boin, Manuel A.; wife, Mary; 7 children; (EK-125)	20 May 1908	K-121
Bond, Alfred; wife, Eleanora	19 Apr. 1862	A-445
Bond, J. L.; wife, M. M.	24 Apr. 1861	A-342
Bond, Joshua L.; M. M.; (F-364, probate, 30 Dec. 1895)	5 May 1873	C-149
Bond, Richard L., married	16 Oct. 1873	C-245
Bond, William H., married	24 May 1873	C-160
Bond, Wm. Hammet, married; (B-396; C-276)	19 May 1866	B-12
Bones, John; wife	10 Dec. 1884	E-528

Applicant and Family Information	Filing Date	Vol.-Pg.
Bonham, B. B.; wife, Bones, Martha M.; (B-134; B-152)	25 Feb. 1861	A-166
Bonnard, Marie; unmarried; two children	22 Oct. 1906	K-7
Bonsell, J. C., married	31 Oct. 1877	D-171
Bonvecchio, Vittorio; wife, Teodora	12 Sep. 1919	L-495
Booth, Edith Griffith; husband, Lorrin; (See L-116)	30 Mar. 1914	L-69
Bopst, Beulah M.; husband, Douglas L.	5 Aug. 1908	K-151
Boquist, Charles V.; wife	21 Sep. 1869	B-352
Borba, Angeline; husband, Emanuel I.	4 Feb. 1907	K-30
Borba, Jennie; Manuel	9 May 1895	H-220
Borda, Gertrude G.; husband, Joseph W.	19 Oct. 1914	L-107
Borer, Eliza H.; John	7 Feb. 1883	E-310
Borgwardt, August; Olina/Oliun	5 Nov. 1889	F-613
Borland, Lee, married	28 Jun. 1872	C-111
Born, J.; wife	18 Nov. 1879	D-489
Boschetti, Pietro; wife, Maria; minor daughter	21 Sep. 1915	L-217
Boss, Henry; wife, Sarah H.	12 Aug. 1910	K-331
Bossa, Margerita; husband, Battista	16 Feb. 1914	L-60
Bostwick, Adelaid L.; husband; 2 children; (E-307); husband requested recording	31 Mar. 1874	C-301
Bosworth, Georgina J.; widow	19 May 1919	L-472
Bosworth, James O., married	30 Jun. 1866	B-21
Bourdens, Lucie; husband, Pierre; (D-552; I-266)	24 Mar. 1880	D-542
Bowden, Elizabeth A., widow of Isaac	5 Mar. 1884	E-446
Bowden, John W., head of family; minor children	30 Aug. 1901	I-352
Bowden, Mary A.; John B.	29 Nov. 1884	E-524
Bowen, J. A.; Ruby E.	17 Jun. 1872	C-106
Bowen, Mary; Frank	16 Aug. 1894	H-91
Bowen, William; Mary; (A-588)	8 Dec. 1860	A-74
Bower, W. G.; wife, Julia M.	5 Jan. 1915	L-130
Bowers, Stella M.; H. P.	21 Feb, 1905	J-55
Bowman, J. F., married	5 Apr. 1878	D-246
Bowman, William F., wife, Rebecca	4 Apr. 1874	C-304
Boyd, Robert S., wife	14 Oct. 1903	I-479
Boyes, H. D.; wife	13 Dec. 1878	D-363
Boyes, John M.; wife, Cora E.	7 Jul. 1916	L-292
Boyes, Lucinda C.; husband, John B.	19 Mar. 1861	A-184
Boyes, Rosina Esther; husband, A. E.	14 Jun. 1920	M-39
Boyes, Sarah F.; John F. "Boyce" in notarization	13 Jul. 1888	F-478

Applicant and Family Information	Filing Date	Vol.-Pg.
Boyle, Catherine; Henry	4 Nov. 1889	F-611
Boyle, Henry; wife, Catharine; (C-10)	12 May 1871	B-517
Brackett, Joanna; J. H.	1 Sep. 1900	I-287
Bradbury, Emaline; John G.	26 Jun. 1871	B-545
Bradlee, Stephen H.; wife	24 Feb. 1880	D-580
Bradley, Hugh; (H-113)	24 Jul. 1894	H-83
Bradshaw, Frances B.; husband, I. A.	14 May 1866	B-10
Bradwick, Albert, married	10 Jul. 1874	B-655
Brady, Sarah, unmarried	4 Aug. 1897	H-598
Brady, William F.; Anna Sophie; child, Helen Marie	26 Dec. 1912	K-477
Brainerd, H. P.; wife; (19 Dec. 1905, J-116)	26 May 1888	F-470
Bramwell, Roland/Rowland; wife	7 Oct. 1879	D-466
Brand, Esther; husband, Meyer; 5 children	4 Sep. 1919	L-492
Brandon, Mynta S.; husband, Herbert A.	27 Mar. 1920	M-25
Brandt, Alonzo B.; wife, Mary E.	9 Jun. 1913	L-8
Brandt, Emma, married	4 Apr. 1874	C-303
Brannum, Muranda; husband, Caswell	20 Dec. 1911	K-405
Bransford, Z. W.; wife	20 May 1884	E-475
Bransford, Zerrel W., married; (E-125)	24 Feb. 1866	A-695
Branstad, Karen Mathea; J. L.	28 Jan. 1893	C-394
Braun, Eliz.; Otto	4 Aug. 1904	J-23
Bray, Frank, married	20 Jun. 1867	B-116
Bray, Wm., single	18 Mar. 1867	B-96
Brayton, Grace L.; husband, William H.	19 Oct. 1916	L-310
Brazill, Margaret; Thomas	28 Sep. 1898	I-122
Brazill, Margaret; husband, Thomas	23 Feb. 1910	K-297
Breans, B. W. K., married	1 Oct. 1872	D-8
Brehm, Marie, Mrs.; husband, Emil	28 Aug. 1916	L-301
Breitenbach, Annie S.; husband, Louis	12 May 1916	L-278
Brennan, Lillian A.; husband, James T.	11 Aug. 1910	K-330
Brennan, Lillie L.; husband, J. J.	9 May 1911	K-377
Bresee, Sylvester B.; wife, Elizabeth	25 Sep. 1863	A-564
Brice, Margaret; William	13 Jul. 1885	F-93
Briemle, Emilie; husband, L.	7 Nov. 1910	K-345
Brigandi, Angelo; wife, Concheta; and children	1 Sep. 1914	L-99
Briggs, Jerome; Elizabeth R.; (I-382)	20 Aug. 1880	E-30
Briggs, Mary E.; Alfred	12 Nov. 1897	I-14
Briggs, Robt. W.; wife, Emoline; (C-263)	3 Jun. 1873	C-165

Applicant and Family Information	Filing Date	Vol.-Pg.
Brigham, G. H., Sr.; wife, Annie M.	4 Jan. 1918	L-391
Brittain, Alva M.; husband, Lester	26 Jan. 1921	M-71
Brittain, Mary Jane; Harvey	12 Oct. 1898	I-132
Brockman, Israel; wife	11 Apr. 1861	A-225
Brockman, Jos. E.; Mary Jane Culbertson Brockman	25 Apr. 1862	A-463
Brockman, Milton; wife, Martha C.; (B-391)	26 Sep. 1864	A-620
Brockman, Virginia M.; husband, Henry M.	6 Jul. 1915	L-189
Brodigan, Nicholas; Bridget	11 May 1867	B-105
Broocke, L. E.; Elvira P.	24 Oct. 1865	A-680
Brooks, Ezra L., married; (C-278; G-437)	13 Jan. 1862	C-37
Brooks, John S.	28 Feb. 1876	C-499
Brooks, Rachel; husband, Ezra D.	4 Feb. 1880	D-514
Brookshire, Elijah; (C-19; C-217)	16 Feb. 1863	A-592
Brothers, Joseph Burgan; wife	30 Jan. 1885	F-19
Brown (Broun), Ella; Frederick T.	9 Oct. 1890	G-127
Brown, A. G.; wife	14 Aug. 1901	I-349
Brown, Alfred; wife	8 May 1886	F-257
Brown, Anna M.; Arthur De W.	4 Sep. 1903	I-466
Brown, Annie St. Clair; J. C.	6 Mar. 1886	F-237
Brown, Cora Belle; husband, Edgar A.	20 Jun. 1919	L-484
Brown, Cordelia A.; J. H.	9 Aug. 1900	I-283
Brown, Dan'l; wife, B. F.	6 Jun. 1885	F-67
Brown, Daniel, married	27 Aug. 1866	B-46
Brown, Diantha R., Mrs.; Frederick W.	4 Feb. 1904	I-494
Brown, E., married	28 Dec. 1871	C-22
Brown, Eliza J.; M. D.; (I-165)	24 Feb. 1897	H-548
Brown, Ella; husband	10 Mar. 1885	F-33
Brown, Emerson; wife, Mary E.	7 Jan. 1915	L-133
Brown, Frank S.; wife	9 Jan. 1901	I-311
Brown, Geo. W.; wife, Mary Elizabeth; minor child, Charles R.	6 May 1912	K-424
Brown, Harriet; Sam'l; probate	16 Feb. 1902	H-141
Brown, Hiram, widower	12 Apr. 1881	E-86
Brown, Ida; husband, Elmo	22 Aug. 1916	L-300
Brown, John; wife; 2 children	18 Apr. 1873	C-145
Brown, Josiah; wife, Anastasie D.; (B-211)	24 Mar. 1864	A-598
Brown, Julia C.; Geo. M.	5 May 1902	I-390
Brown, L. W., married	22 Apr. 1861	A-356
Brown, Maria Jose; Frank S.	28 Feb. 1885	F-28

Applicant and Family Information	Filing Date	Vol.-Pg.
Brown, Marie, Mrs.; Geo. S.	8 Feb. 1899	I-177
Brown, Martha; Judson	5 Sep. 1896	H-484
Brown, Mary Ellen; Horace E.	30 Mar. 1900	I-262
Brown, Mortlock; wife, Mary	7 Jan. 1909	K-196
Brown, Ruth; husband, W. R.	31 Dec. 1914	L-128
Brown, T. P.; wife; 5 children	6 May 1905	J-69
Brown, W. R.; wife, Ruth	17 July 1913	L-13
Brown, Wm. M.; May M.	30 Mar. 1903	I-441
Brown, Wm.; wife	13 Feb. 1879	D-381
Browne, Eliza, Wm.	31 Jan. 1898	I-49
Browne, R. S., head of family; 1 minor child	10 Feb. 1897	H-534
Bruer, Gertrude O.; husband, Fred M.	19 May 1913	L-176
Brumfield, Geo. P.; Anna	30 Mar. 1861	A-198
Brumfield, Thomas; wife	14 Feb. 1870	B-380
Bruner, Anna E.; widow, alone	12 Dec. 1904	J-47
Bruning, Christopher H. W.; Amanda	24 Jun. 1902	I-398
Bruns, Adolph Herman; Auguste	29 Apr. 1861	A-362
Brusa, Paolo; wife, Josephone; 8 children	31 Oct. 1905	J-120
Brush, D. C., married	30 Dec. 1873	C-273
Brush, Geo. M.; wife; (H-505)	18 Apr. 1895	H-211
Brush, Julia A.; husband, J. H.	23 Oct. 1918	L-443
Brush, Lena G.; husband, Frank A.	15 Oct. 1918	L-437
Brush, Rachel A., married	13 Sep. 1867	B-149
Bryan, C. W.; wife	17 Aug. 1899	I-215
Bryan, C. W.; wife	17 Aug. 1899	I-215
Bryan, Joseph P. Hilda; Joseph, a minor	21 Dec. 1912	K-476
Bryant, Allen, wife	22 May 1889	F-567
Bryant, Bettie; husband, Allen	2 Jul. 1913	L-12
Bryant, Fannie E.; W. J.	4 May 1882	E-211
Bryant, L. Upham, Mrs.; husband	16 Apr. 1883	E-322
Bryant, Louisa T.; husband, Charles G.	8 Aug. 1912	K-441
Bryant, Margaret J.; Andrew J.	10 May 1883	E-331
Bryant, Susan E.; W. H.	18 Jan. 1905	J-52
Bryant, Thomas H.; wife	30 Sep. 1880	E-142
Bryant, Wm. S.; L. W.	15 Sep. 1871	B-559
Bryant, Wm. C.; wife, Ann	26 Oct. 1860	A-46
Buckland, Leonard H.; wife	11 Jun. 1881	E-102
Buckle, Julia Etta; Thomas	8 Feb. 1884	E-435

Applicant and Family Information	Filing Date	Vol.-Pg.
Buckmaster, Solomon; wife; (G-189, insolvent debtor)	10 Jul. 1884	E-486
Budd, E. R.; wife, Adaline S.	16 Oct. 1860	A-36
Bugbee, Elnora A.; Norman	24 Aug. 1887	F-411
Bugbee. Eva May; 1 minor	6 Jul. 1915	L-192
Bull, Jennie, widow	16 Jul. 1895	H-240
Bullard, Wm. P.; wife, Adaline M.	19 Jun. 1869	B-335
Bumbaugh, E. A., Mrs.; husband	5 Aug. 1885	F-106
Bumbaugh, Emma A.; C. M.	17 Sep. 1903	I-467
Bunch, Martin; wife, Mary E.	18 Jan. 1864	A-584
Burbank, Caleb; wife, Charlotte F.	6 Jul. 1871	B-550
Burch, Geo. W.; wife	7 Feb. 190	I-244
Burdick, J. D.; wife	17 Jan. 1884	E-421
Burel, Emilie; husband, Joseph; Arthur, 14; Josephine, 12; Eloise, 10; Eugenie, 8; Emilie, 5; Alice	13 Nov. 1906	K-18
Burgess, Rybert John	17 Oct. 1918	L-438
Burgett, Eliz.; Wm.	27 Mar. 1902	I-420
Burghard, Gustavus F.; wife	17 Nov. 1900	I-306
Burke, Margaret; husband, Thomas; adult children: Mary L., Chas A.; Thomas, Jr.; Cathcrine; Agnes, and James (minor)	24 Aug. 1891	E-208
Burnett, A. J., widower; probate	16 Apr. 1887	F-387
Burnett, John H.; wife	2 Dec. 1884	E-525
Burnett, Mary C., widow; 1 minor	14 Sep. 1908	K-165
Burnett, Wm., married	14 Sep. 1866	B-47
Burnett, Wm.; C.	15 Nov. 1870	B-469
Burney, John; wife	20 Nov. 1883	E-402
Burnham, A. E.; wife	6 Jun. 1885	F-71
Burns, Elisa; Peter	16 Aug. 1882	E-255
Burns, Johanna; husband, George; no children	20 Jan. 1921	M-68
Burns, Lizzie L.; Lewis A.	9 Oct. 1900	I-296
Burr, Isabel D.; Frank	26 Sep. 1903	I-473
Burris, Laura M.; husband, Luther W.	2 Jun. 1909	K-232
Burris, Wm.; wife, Elizabeth	15 Nov. 1860	A-52
Burroughs, R. E.; wife	25 Nov. 1902	I-421
Burrus, Geo. W.; wife	1 Jul. 1878	D-283
Burus, Anna J.; Eugene F.	24 Oct. 1890	G-139
Bush, H. N.; wife, Maria I.; 2 children	4 Jun. 1906	J-134
Bushnell, Amasa, married	9 May 1863	A-553
Buster, Francis Marion; Melinda Elizabeth	21 Mar. 1868	B-212
Butler, (Buttler) Mary; Frank	8 Apr. 1882	E-203

Applicant and Family Information	Filing Date	Vol.-Pg.
Butler, Ann E.	15 Jan. 1908	K-93
Butler, Caroline H.; Francisco	19 Sep. 1891	C-232
Butler, James, married	31 Aug. 1872	B-599
Butler, Jesse L.; (see "Patents")	12 Aug. 1903	I-228
Butler, Joanna L.; husband, A. J.	24 Apr. 1861	A-308
Butler, Thos. J.; wife	21 Oct. 1886	F-318
Butler, Wm. A.; wife, Margaret F.; (A-312)	3 Jan. 1861	A-96
Butt, Alfred; wife	7 Nov. 1890	G-142
Button, Betsey M., married; family	10 Nov. 1875	C-456
Button, Ellen H.; I. V.	26 Oct. 1893	G-476
Button, Isaac V., married	11 Oct. 1866	B-24
Butts, Margaret; husband, T. J.	2 Jul. 1912	K-433
Butts, Mary R.; David C.	6 May 1884	E-465
Byers, Emma E.; husband, W. A.; (8 Nov. 1915, L-228)	24 Jul. 1915	L-197
Byrne, Amelia F.; husband, Malichy; probate	23 Jan. 1895	F-219
Byrne, M., married; (E-108; G-427)	3 Oct. 1877	D-159
Byrum, B., Mrs.	3 Sep. 1910	K-332

Applicant and Family Information	Filing Date	Vol.-Pg.
Cadden, Thomas; wife	4 Feb. 1888	F-454
Cadwell, A.; wife (I-65)	23 Jul. 1896	H-464
Cain, M. J., Mrs., widow	24 Jul. 1896	H-467
Caldeira, Maria; Manuel S. A.	6 Apr. 1914	L-70
Calder, Ethel R.; husband, Geo. W.	25 Nov. 1912	K-472
Calder, Sarah A., Mrs.; Alexander, dec'd., probate (8 Feb. 1889, D-474)	7 Nov. 1881	E-156
Caldwell, A. J., head of family	25 May 1883	E-338
Caldwell, F. M., married	28 Jul. 1873	C-208
Call, William L., head of family; mother; sister & sister's children, 4	6 Sep. 1893	G-459
Callahan, Ellen J.; John	30 Oct. 1894	H-104
Camm, William; wife, Hannah (F-182)	25 Apr. 1871	B-508
Camp, Eliza J.; Guy R. (G-236)	29 Jul. 1891	G-207
Campau, Louise H.; George	12 Jun. 1907	K-52
Campbell, H. R.; wife, Bessie Wyman Campbell	9 Jun. 1902	I-395
Campbell, Henry, wife	20 Oct. 1879	D-476
Campbell, James; Sarah E.	7 Mar. 1918	L-400
Campbell, John W.; Matilda C.	12 Apr. 1864	A-601
Campbell, Joseph, wife	19 Oct. 1896	H-494
Campbell, Matilda L.; husband, John	22 Jan. 1864	A-587
Campbell, Talbert T., married	13 Dec. 1873	C-264
Campion, Thomas, widower	12 Mar. 1887	F-368
Camron, David E.; minor brothers: Alva O.; William W.	9 Mar. 1861	A-143
Canan, W. S.; H. E.	8 Feb. 1861	A-126
Canan, Wm. S.; wife, Mary A.	9 May 1872	C-95
Cane, Wm.; widower; child	13 Jan. 1873	B-626
Caneveri, Giovanni, widower; 5 children; wife, d. Sept. 1903	25 Jan. 1904	I-492
Canfield, Wm. D.; Sally Ann	21 Apr. 1862	A-452
Cannon, John M., married	18 Feb. 1861	A-135
Cannon, Mary Ann, widow	2 Apr. 1869	B-321
Cantoni, Augustina; Romeo	8 Apr. 1918	L-406
Capell, Sarah A.; B. B.	13 Jun. 1887	F-396
Capra, Rosa; Chas.	13 Feb. 1900	I-245
Capucetti, L. A.; wife (I-326; G-181)	8 Oct. 1897	H-636
Cardana, Katie; John	11 Jul. 1893	G-430
Carder, D. D.; Mary C. (B-189)	20 Apr. 1861	A-295
Cardinet, Adolph, widower	22 Mar. 1889	F-540
Cardoza, F. J.; wife	14 Jan. 1901	I-313

Applicant and Family Information	Filing Date	Vol.-Pg.
Carey, C., Mrs., widow	29 May 1885	F-63
Carey, James C.; wife	7 Dec. 1885	E-554
Carico, Effie; J. W., Dr.	9 Oct. 1909	K-271
Carithers, Mary E.; David N.	8 Jun. 1889	F-575
Carlson, Amanda; husband, Albin	8 Apr. 1913	K-496
Carlson, Katherine C.; Wm., a widower	15 Nov. 1915	L-230
Carlton, Columbus; Nellie H.	23 Apr. 1864	A-604
Carlyon Eliz. J.; Thos.	21 Feb. 1899	I-187
Carothers, William O., married	30 Aug. 1871	B-541
Carr, Alice P.; Chas. F.	1 Aug. 1895	H-249
Carriger, C. C., insolvent debtor, probate	11 Sep. 1895	F-309
Carriger, Kate, Mrs., head of family, unmarried; sister, Nellie C. O'Brien	26 Aug. 1903	I-464
Carriger, Lizzie J.; Caleb	12 Mar. 1885	F-35
Carriger, Mary A.; Nicholas	29 Jun. 1885	F-84
Carrillo, Elizabeth Meyer; husband, Manuel, dec;d; 3 minor children; m. 20 Dec. 1894, Sonoma Co.; Manuel, d. 14 July 1906	10 Dec. 1906	K-22
Carrillo, Joaquin N.; wife, Guadalupe	1 Mar. 1865	A-640
Carrillo, Joaquin, married	21 Feb. 1876	C-496
Carrillo, Joaquin; Mary (D-93; F-596; E-312)	16 Jul. 1870	B-430
Carrillo, Julio; Theodaco	14 Nov. 1863	A-571
Carrillo, Martha; Jose; J. B.	13 Nov. 1882	E-283
Carrillo, Mary E.; H. G.	27 Jun. 1883	E-348
Carrillo, Nellie I.; Lee Arthur	27 Apr. 1917	L-344
Carrillo, Theodosia; Julio	8 Dec. 1888	F-537
Carrington, Lola E.; Bartine	26 Jul. 1915	L-198
Carrington, Mary E.; Chas. N.	26 Sep. 1890	G-119
Carrington, Paul T.; Clara D.	16 Aug. 1915	L-204
Carson, Dorothy E., married	2 Nov. 1874	C-345
Carson, Robert W.; Mary A.	9 Jan. 1865	A-634
Carswell, Harriet L.; Geo. W. (H-17)	26 Sep. 1892	G-348
Carter, Ellen; husband, John A.	19 Sep. 1874	C-332
Carter, Esther N.; L. W.	22 Oct. 1910	K-340
Carter, Harriet E., married	24 Nov. 1873	C-258
Carter, J. W.; wife	2 Oct. 1903	I-475
Carter, John M.; wife	7 Dec. 1894	H-122
Carter, Landon; Susan (A-626)	19 Jul. 1860	A-4
Carter, O. W.; married; family	7 Jul. 1877	C-569

Applicant and Family Information	Filing Date	Vol.-Pg.
Cartwright, Helen; Chas. F.	25 Sep. 1915	L-218
Cary, Frank L.; wife	2 Sep. 1884	E-505
Case, Adelaide L.; G. W.	4 Mar. 1878	D-226
Case, Austin B.; Harriet	22 Apr. 1861	A-359
Caselli, Antonio; Clotilde (saloon in Freestone)	27 Jan. 1899	I-169
Casey, Aileen L.; Hiram E.	20 Jan. 1921	M-69
Casey, Julia A.; Levy J.	30 Sep. 1881	E-143
Casey, Kate, widow of Jeremiah/Jerry, d. 9 Apr. 1895; homestead applied for 22 Nov. 1872 (B-609)	19 Apr. 1904	J-11
Cassagnes, Auguste; Virginie	1 May 1918	L-408
Casseris, Elise, Mrs.; husband, Francisco	14 Sep. 1868	B-265
Cassidy, J. W.; wife, L. L. (A-215)	10 Jan. 1861	A-104
Casson, E. T.; wife, Florence M. (L-441)	22 Jul. 1912	K-439
Castex, Constance; husband, Andrew; 2 children	2 Jul. 1912	K-435
Catelani, Mary; Leonoro	13 Dec. 1915	L-240
Catlin, Elon, married	15 Apr. 1869	B-326
Catron, William C.; Elizabeth (B-381)	11 Nov. 1862	A-519
Caulfield, Thomas, married	30 Dec. 1878	D-369
Cavanagh, Catharine,; husband, Joseph	21 May 1867	B-118
Caverly, Orin; wife	25 Feb. 1880	D-533
Cerri, Rosa; Romeo	4 Mar. 1921	M-77
Chadbourne, Josephine M.; S. W.	21 Aug. 1890	G-93
Chadd, George H., unmarried; 2 minor children	13 Nov. 1915	L-229
Challen, Joseph; Auguste Laal Challen	15 Dec. 1861	A-125
Chamberlain, Corinthia A.; Albert F.	23 Sep. 1903	I-471
Chamberlain, J. R.; Luella	9 May 1911	K-376
Chambers, Paulina; husband, G. K.	10 Aug. 1875	C-428
Chambers, Thomas; wife, Hannah	2 Jun. 1865	A-651
Champion, Mary A.; John	3 Dec. 1892	G-378
Champlain, Margaret, married	19 Dec. 1870	B-476
Chandler, Alice C.; Rollon O.	22 Jun. 1895	H-231
Chaney, Thomas, widower	4 Apr. 1887	F-384
Chapman, Elizabeth; W. W.	19 Sep. 1887	F-417
Chartrand, Mary E.; A. E.	7 Jul. 1906	J-141
Chase, Charlote, unmarried	3 Sep. 1908	K-161
Chase, Dudley; Sarah G.	1 Apr. 1862	A-417
Chase, Ina E.; C. F.	24 Jan. 1916	L-251
Chase, Martha E.	30 Aug. 1895	H-273

Applicant and Family Information	Filing Date	Vol.-Pg.
Cheda, Pietro; wife	22 Aug. 1896	H-471
Cheeney, Edward H.; Sarah; (Edw. d. 6 Jul. 1889; probate; D-488)	6 Jan. 1868	B-181
Chelini, Lucia; husband, A.; 3 minor children	5 Jan. 1914	L-53
Cheney, Lillie M.; Thos. H.	2 Sep. 1895	H-275
Chenoweth, James M.; wife	7 Dec. 1891	G-281
Chenoweth, Miles H., unmarried	4 Apr. 1861	A-203
Chiappari, Joseph; Catherine	25 Jan. 1910	K-289
Childers, Alonzo, married (C-55; D-281; D-70)	22 Aug. 1876	C-550
Childers, Spencer, married	28 Jun. 1878	D-279
Chiles, Alda W.; Wm. G.	21 Mar. 1894	H-37
Chiotti, Tilly; husband, James	10 Oct. 1912	K-459
Chisholm, Annie C.; Wm.	16 Mar. 1891	G-173
Christiansen, C. P.; Theresa A.	25 Apr. 1916	L-271
Christianson, Carl	21 Apr. 1877	D-112
Christianson, H. B., widower	12 Sep. 1883	E-377
Christie, John B., married	4 Oct. 1873	C-232
Christlich, Henrietta; (Frederick dec'd., probate)	9 Jul. 1888	D-431
Church, Cynthia J.; Samuel H.	9 Aug. 1880	E-24
Church, Grace D.; A. P.	26 Oct. 1910	K-342
Churchman, Wm.; 1 daughter over 18; 2 sons, 2 daughters, minors (B-386; C-81)	28 Oct. 1860	B-361
Churchman, Wm.; Martha M. (B-274)	18 Jan. 1865	A-636
Clanton, David C.; wife	7 Apr. 1882	E-201
Clapp, Ruth Ann; husband, George H., Dr.	17 May 1880	D-573
Clark, Albert; wife, Mary Jane	31 Oct. 1866	B-71
Clark, Annie; John Alexander	26 Feb. 1917	L-335
Clark, Antoinette Hill, now unmarried; one child	7 May 1892	G-315
Clark, Bessie K.; James E.	17 Oct. 1918	L-439
Clark, Byron; wife	23 Jan. 1882	E-178
Clark, Emma L.; W. L.	21 Jul. 1915	L-196
Clark, Ethel	8 Mar. 1921	M-78
Clark, Fannie L.; husband	31 Dec. 1887	F-439
Clark, Fannie E., head of family; 2 minor children (E-327) husband dec'd.	6 Feb. 1882	E-188
Clark, Frances U.; Wm. S., dec'd., probate	26 Jan. 1898	G-90
Clark, Frederick W.; Margaret E.; Estelle; Gertrude	23 Jun. 1896	H-444
Clark, James L., married	15 Jun. 1875	D-22
Clark, James H. H., Mrs.; wife of	11 Jan. 1908	K-91

Applicant and Family Information	Filing Date	Vol.-Pg.
Clark, John E.; wife, Nancy; 2 children	31 Jul. 1877	C-587
Clark, Marinda Jennette; Stephen D.	10 Dec. 1903	I-486
Clark, Mary; Michael	29 Dec. 1897	I-33
Clark, Mary; husband; 4 children (F-167)	9 Nov. 1885	F-159
Clark, Patrick; wife, Rosa Ann	13 Jul. 1875	C-418
Clark, W. L.; wife	15 Oct. 1897	H-639
Clary, Christie Temple; Paul D.	12 Jul. 1918	L-413
Clary, John A.; Isabella D.	19 Feb. 1868	B-186
Clemens, F. H.; Mary	28 Jul. 1886	F-292
Clement, Gilbert H.; Emily M.	4 Jan. 1868	B-303
Clements, Annie; Mathew (L-426)	2 May 1910	K-316
Clippinger, Levo E.; wife, Grover C.	12 May 1916	L-277
Clough, Julia M., widow of M. A.	8 Jul. 1915	L-193
Cnopius, Johan, married	10 Nov. 1876	D-53
Cobb, Guy L.; wife, Cynthia Cobb	1 Aug. 1874	C-320
Cobb, Jessie Haskell; husband, George O.	8 Oct. 1913	L-37
Coburn, W. R., married	16 Jan. 1868	B-183
Cockrill, Martha D.; Bruce T.	30 Aug. 1888	F-498
Codding, G. R., married (D-179)	23 Apr. 1868	B-228
Codding, M. M., Mrs.; Geo. R., dec'd.	18 Jul. 1896	H-459
Cody, Matthew; wife	16 Mar. 1887	F-372
Cofer, George W.; Nancy	10 Nov. 1866	B-75
Cofer, P. J., Mrs., married	12 Jun. 1875	C-408
Coffey, America Ellen; Jas. H.	7 Apr. 1896	H-398
Coffey, Chas. H.; Maggie C.	24 Mar. 1894	H-39
Coffey, J. H.; wife	19 Jun. 1892	G-294
Coffey, Nellie; Sam'l A.	17 Aug. 1895	H-259
Coffey, S. A.; Nellie	24 Aug. 1905	J-94
Cohn, Isaac H., married	15 May 1866	B-11
Cole, Charles B.; wife	26 Jul. 1893	G-439
Cole, Emily M.; Henry L.	11 Sep. 1906	J-154
Cole, Grace; Isaac T.	21 Aug. 1907	K-68
Cole, Mary E.; A. C.	18 Feb. 1896	H-384
Cole, Priscilla; J. H.	21 Aug. 1894	H-93
Cole, S. A., Mrs., widow, head of family	24 Jun. 1891	G-200
Coleman, Elena E.; James	2 Nov. 1895	H-309
Colgan, Bertha; A. L.	20 May 1915	L-178
Colgan, Mollie E., Edward P.	12 May 1890	G-38

Applicant and Family Information	Filing Date	Vol.-Pg.
Colli, Domenico; Ernestine	11 Feb. 1914	L-59
Collings, Louisa A.; A. F.	1 Jul. 1898	I-95
Collins, Alice L.; Charles S.	19 Jun. 1889	F-584
Collins, Barbara Ann; husband, George	17 Nov. 1879	D-488
Collins, James W.; Mary	1 May 1875	C-391
Collins, Mary B.; J. W.	19 Jun. 1901	I-338
Collins, Stephen, single	21 Apr. 1879	D-404
Collister, Stanley W.; wife	7 Mar. 1902	I-380
Colson, Marie; John	31 Jan. 1895	H-150
Colton, F. D.; Submit	8 Feb. 1869	B-312
Colton, Lois A.; Joseph P.	13 Dec. 1900	I-308
Colvin, Thomas S.; married	23 Jul. 1873	C-198
Colwell, Caroline E.; husband, Edwin B. (E-334)	15 Jun. 1880	D-583
Colwell, Charlotte A.; Harry C.	28 Sep. 1908	K-170
Comerford, Richard; Sarah, probate	24 Mar. 1890	D-540
Commary, Prudent; Julia A. Burleson Commary (B-206)	16 Apr. 1861	A-232
Commins, Edward, head of family	29 Sep. 1862	A-508
Compere, Mary, widow of Iowa A.	4 Feb. 1909	K-206
Compton, Emma L.; Theodore J.	10 Oct. 1918	L-440
Congrove, Jonathan; Mary A.	4 Sep. 1890	A-21
Congrove, Lucy J.; J.	13 Mar. 1878	D-233
Conklin, Charles; wife	14 Jan. 1885	F-16
Conlan, Amelia; Wm.	28 Dec. 1909	K-290
Conniff, John; Bridget (E-558; F-278)	1 Feb. 1881	E-72
Conniff, T. E.; Josephine	18 Apr. 1908	K-119
Connolly, Bernard J.; wife	15 Feb. 1895	H-172
Connolly, John D.; Georgina G.	5 Jun. 1906	J-133
Connolly, M. W., married	7 Apr. 1877	D-103
Connolly, M. W., single, insolvent	6 Dec. 1878	E-2
Connolly, Minnie A.; husband	11 Jan. 1881	D-62
Connor, Judith E.; E. P.	9 May 1884	E-467
Conroy, Margaret; Peter	20 Jun. 1867	B-124
Consani, Cristina; Alfredo	4 Feb. 1915	L-141
Conway, John, married	16 Nov. 1874	C-341
Cook, Barbara F.; husband, James	9 Jul. 1879	D-431
Cook, Basha P.,; Isaac Newton	1 Nov. 1902	I-418
Cook, Carrie L.; C. H.	14 Aug. 1897	H-610
Cook, Eliza; Isaac F.	29 Jan. 1886	F-212

Applicant and Family Information	Filing Date	Vol.-Pg.
Cook, G. A., married	4 Apr. 1866	B-5
Cook, George M.; wife, Mary Ann	4 Jan. 1873	B-623
Cook, Herbert E.; Susan (D-198)	6 Aug. 1875	C-427
Cook, James H.	2 Jun. 1892	G-318
Cook, John; Margaret (B-348; D-271)	1 Feb. 1866	A-694
Cook, Kathryn M.; C. C.	23 Jan. 1919	L-457
Cook, Mary Jane; Israel/Isarel	7 Nov. 1902	I-419
Cook, Pearl M.; Fred B.	31 Jul. 1906	J-145
Cook, Rebecca; Thos. G.	5 Jun. 1919	L-478
Cook, Richard; Louise	27 Mar. 1920	M-26
Coolbroth, S. W.; wife	20 Dec. 1876	D-61
Cooley, J. S.; wife, Sarah (F-226; M-72)	29 Jan. 1886	F-208
Coon, Hannah A. nee Norris; P. C.	24 Jul. 1895	H-245
Coon, Lydia A., Mrs.; Robt. W.	9 Dec. 1880	E-52
Coon, Mary E.; L. O.	13 Sep. 1893	G-462
Cooper, Betsy M., Mrs.; husband, H. H. (B-235)	4 Jan. 1864	A-580
Cooper, Fannie Josephine; Thomas S.	6 Jun. 1891	E-620
Cooper, Hannah, widow; Guy, Hazel, minors; John, intestate 3/27/07	3 Jun. 1907	K-49
Cooper, Lizzie; Thos. J.	18 Jan. 1904	I-491
Cooper, S. V.; 2 minor children	1 Dec. 1886	F-333
Cooper, Susan L.; James R.	17 Dec. 1902	I-424
Coops, Johanne C.; Jonathan H.	24 May 1905	J-72
Cope, L. L., Mrs., widow	15 Nov. 1878	D-354
Copeland, William L.; wife	19 Apr. 1882	E-210
Coppin, Estelle; Albert	15 Sep. 1908	K-167
Corbin, Francis B., married	20 Mar. 1884	E-452
Corbin, Geo. H.; wife	4 Aug. 1891	G-212
Corippo, Celestine; P.	6 Jan. 1905	J-50
Corley, Rhoda H.; Geo. A.	17 Jun. 1908	K-134
Corman, Claudia E.; Franklin P.	14 May 1904	J-8
Cornelison, Frances (F-339; I-275)	1 Sep. 1896	F-305
Corria, Antone F.; wife, Heter, dec'd.; her minor children Geo. Robbins	19 Nov. 1912	K-469
Corrick, Mabel Ella; A. R.	25 Oct. 1918	L-445
Corry, Constance; Frederick J.	29 Jun. 1909	K-242
Corville, Maria; Emerson	15 Oct. 1883	E-391
Costello, Bridget M.; husband	16 Dec. 1864	A-632
Costello, Thomas; Rose; Stephen, Francis, minors; probate	16 Dec. 1889	D-512

Applicant and Family Information	Filing Date	Vol.-Pg.
Coster, Rilla; George	24 Feb. 1909	K-210
Costly, Anna; married	4 Dec. 1875	C-461
Coul, Annie C., married, head of family	26 Jun. 1878	D-274
Coulter, Joseph H., married	10 Sep. 1877	D-145
Coulter, Rachel M.; S. Y.	22 Dec. 1886	F-343
Coulter, Sterling T.; Rachel M.	27 Apr. 1861	A-348
Courtney, Patrick, single	21 Feb. 1884	E-443
Covet, Louis; Francise Josephine	11 Oct. 1895	H-292
Cowan, Joseph F.; wife	28 Aug. 1905	J-95
Cox, A. J.; aged mother; minors	9 Feb. 1876	C-490
Cox, Fathy A.; husband, Jordan (A-685; B-334)	12 Aug. 1863	A-562
Cox, Ida J.; N. H.	29 Aug. 1892	G-341
Cox, J. Bradford, married	30 Mar. 1872	C-73
Cozzens, Richard; wife	5 Jul. 1879	D-430
Crabtree, Melissa A.; head of family	10 Feb. 1904	I-497
Craig, Oliver W.; Sophia T. (F.); [(O. W., dec'd 8/4/1892, probate, (E-394)]; no children; probate	6 Jun. 1862	A-493
Craine, Eliza J., married	24 Apr. 1876	C-516
Craine, Thomas, married	29 Jul. 1865	A-665
Cralle, Nancy J.; L. J.	9 Oct. 1889	E-595
Cramer, D. R.; wife	17 Mar. 1891	G-175
Cramer, Fannie L.; John F.	30 Mar. 1906	J-128
Cramer, Henry D.; Anita; no children	12 Mar. 1912	K-417
Cramer, John; wife	9 Jan. 1891	G-158
Crandall, George N.; Amanda F.	17 Sep. 1860	A-25
Crane, Geo. L.; Harriet (C-576)	12 Nov. 1869	B-364
Crane, Harriet; husband, George L.	20 Jul. 1877	C-576
Crane, Joel; Jane E.	20 Nov. 1860	A-55
Crane, Josiah H., married	31 Jan. 1871	B-499
Crane, Tarleton Lee; wife, Mary (G-114)	22 Sep. 1886	E-560
Crawford, Adam, married (E-567; H-419)	28 Jun. 1873	C-182
Crawford, C. H.; Emma	5 Feb. 1909	K-207
Crawford, John; Julia	23 Apr. 1861	A-313
Crawford, Mary J.; husband, Thomas	3 Aug. 1871	B-534
Crayne, Margaret; Allen	16 Jan. 1914	L-55
Creagh, Michael; wife	17 Mar. 1882	E-197
Creighton,Thomas, married (E-39; E-550)	19 Sep. 1874	C-329
Crewdson, Angeline L.; G. F.	13 Jun. 1889	F-580

Applicant and Family Information	Filing Date	Vol.-Pg.
Crilly, Ellen F., widow	1 Jun. 1886	F-267
Crilly, N.; wife, Ellen	8 Sep. 1870	B-445
Crippen, Harriet M.; (Perry dec'd 12/23/1889; probate, D-520)	5 Apr. 1884	E-457
Crist, Mrs. W. K.; W. K.	19 Aug. 1898	I-108
Crist, Rhoda; Wm. (G-398)	5 May 1885	F-48
Crist, Wm.; Rosana	13 Feb. 1867	B-87
Crocker, Harry B.; wife	4 Apr. 1903	I-444
Crocker, James, married	1 Sep. 1868	B-258
Crofs, J. D.; Sarah	25 Apr. 1861	A-330
Crosby, Archibald R.; Nettie D.	8 Sep. 1919	L-493
Crosby, J. C.; Sarah J.	15 Feb. 1886	F-231
Crose, John M., married	20 Nov. 1878	D-356
Crose, Mary; John M.	4 Jun. 1896	H-434
Crowell, Wm. H.; Jane	31 Dec. 1860	A-94
Crozier, George; Elma; Geo., 15; Leslie S., 13; Alice, 10; Olive, 6	22 Jan. 1915	L-135
Crystal, Carl; wife	10 Feb. 1910	K-296
Crystal, Elicia M.; B. F.	13 Sep. 1895	H-286
Cuicello, Frank L.; wife, Pearl J.; 3 minor children (K-375)	3 Dec. 1915	L-236
Cuicello, Rosalind; Manuel G.	12 Apr. 1910	K-311
Cummings, Caroline; husband, William; probate	15 Jun. 1891	E-173
Cummings, John; wife	20 Jul. 1883	E-354
Cummings, Mary J.; Eli R.	1 Feb. 1897	H-528
Cummings, Sarah; Harry W.	21 Mar. 1904	J-6
Cummings, Susan A.; J. S.	13 Jun. 1900	I-275
Cummins, Malinda B.; Thilson P.	4 Mar. 1918	L-399
Cummins, Martha Nina; Geo. A. (L-410)	19 Nov. 1909	K-278
Cunningham, Susan J.; John	29 Sep. 1887	F-419
Cunninghame, Alice O.; Wm. J. (Cunningham in notarization); (K-177)	6 Aug. 1897	H-602
Currier, Susan C.; children Maggie	8 Jun. 1874	C-311
Currier, William, widower (I-155)	24 Oct. 1894	G-509
Curry, Ellen W.; Patrick	4 Apr. 1877	D-102
Curry, John, Mrs.; John	15 Jun. 1891	G-196
Curry, Margaret; husband, John; her minor children; probate	4 Mar. 1895	F-238
Curti, Vincenzo; Santina	3 Jul. 1916	L-289
Curtis, Ezra M.; wife, Ellen M.	5 Sep. 1876	C-551
Curtiss, Thomas Edson; wife	13 Oct. 1903	I-478

Applicant and Family Information Name	Filing Date	Vol.-Pg.
Dabner, Isabella F. Silva; Tony	28 Dec. 1912	K-478
Dabney, C. W.; May M.	27 Feb. 1908	K-102
Daddi, Virginia; Ferdinando	15 Aug. 1892	G-334
Daly, Bartholomen, married	2 May 1870	B-401
Daly, Hannah, unmarried	26 Feb. 1877	D-88
Damon, E. Charles; wife	18 Oct. 1882	E-276
Damon, Maggie A.; M. H.	23 Sep. 1907	K-75
Damsell, Stella A.; Josephus	15 Mar. 1916	L-263
Daneri, Henry, unmarried	15 Nov. 1910	K-348
Daniels, Christina L.; daughter Lucile B., 6 mo. (Frederick dec'd)	30 Aug. 1909	K-254
Daniels, Fannie J.; Roy A.	1 Aug. 1911	K-383
Daniels, Sarah L.; (Newell dec'd)	1 Oct. 1904	J-35
Darby, Josie; J. D.	12 May 1908	K-123
Dardis, Lida; A.	6 Sep. 1880	E-34
Darrow, Dolly; husband, W. H.	31 Mar. 1879	D-397
Darrow, John O.; Mary E.	4 Jan. 1867	B-62
Daugherty, Jno.; wife	29 Jan. 1881	E-68
Daugherty, John W.; wife, Clementine	7 Jan. 1862	A-393
Daughhetee, Daniel P., married	16 May 1867	B-110
Davidson, Alex T.; wife	30 Sep. 1881	E-141
Davidson, Anne; husband	28 Jul. 1879	D-441
Davidson, George, head of family	20 Jan. 1880	D-506
Davies, Thomas C.; wife, Fannie C.; abandonment	3 Nov. 1860	A-54&
Davis, A. G. W.; wife	31 May 1879	D-417
Davis, A.; Jenne	7 Jan. 1878	D-194
Davis, Elizabeth; Chas. N.	7 Nov. 1904	J-43
Davis, Emma M.; Erastus L.	10 Feb. 1908	K-96
Davis, Geo. B.; wife	15 Jan. 1889	F-529
Davis, Hannah; husband, Jonathan	21 Sep. 1861	A-380
Davis, Ida Orcelia; husband, Charles N.	19 Jun. 1919	L-483
Davis, John B., married	19 Apr. 1877	D-108
Davis, Jonathan, insolvent debtor	18 May 1863	A-555
Davis, Josephine M.; Ulysses G. (4/22/1909; K-225)	15 Aug. 1907	K-67
Davis, Mary E. Ore	14 Dec. 1915	L-242
Davis, Mary Ann; husband, A. G.	7 Dec. 1872	B-613
Davis, Mary E.; husband, D. O. (9/21/1883; E-397)	28 Mar. 1879	D-400
Davis, Mary E.; Erastus L.	27 Jan. 1914	L-58
Davis, Mary E.; J. E., dec'd	21 May 1908	K-126
Davis, Rebecca E.; W. W.	10 Aug. 1892	G-332
Davis, Sarah; husband, W. K.	9 Jun. 1868	B-241
Davis, Solon W.; Julia A.	18 Jun. 1908	K-133

Applicant and Family Information Name	Filing Date	Vol.-Pg.
Davis. Ira; wife, Catharine (C-462)	5 Aug. 1867	B-135
Dawkins, Richard W.; Annie	30 Mar. 1907	K-39
Day, Edwin; wife, (also E-153)	12 May 1880	E-13
Deal, George, married	31 Jan. 1880	E-8
Deane-Morgan, R. F.; Charlotte	6 Dec. 1912	K-475
DeCarly, Modesta; J. B.	14 Nov. 1898	I-145
Decker, Margaret H.; husband, Henry	9 Apr. 1873	B-637
Dehay, Marie; Armand	18 Jul. 1889	F-598
Delanoy, Mary F.; Fred N.; children: Mary Florence, Frederick Wm., Austin B.	16 Aug. 1888	F-488
DeLatimer, Beulah; Walter V.	13 Jul. 1914	L-91
Delehanty, Patrick; Ellen (Delehenty)	26 Nov. 1879	D-493
DeMartini, Victor; Lena	29 Aug. 1917	L-366
DeMello, Rosa; Manuel Estracia	10 Oct. 1918	L-434
Demetz, Mrs. Anna; Henry (Demitz in declaration)	26 Dec. 1885	F-180
Dempsey, Ann; James	22 Mar. 1895	H-198
Dennes, E. F.; wife	31 Aug. 1904	J-31
Denning, Julia A., widow	7 Feb. 1890	G-9
Dennison, E. D.; wife, Ethel S.; 1 child	1 Nov. 1920	M-54
Densmore, Geo. F.; wife	6 Feb. 1886	F-221
DeRosa, Louisa; Manuel	17 Jul. 1894	H-78
DeRose, Mary; Antone	18 Oct. 1909	K-273
DeRose, Rosa; Joseph P.	21 Apr. 1891	G-183
DeSomoza, V, Maria; hus. Fernando (Note: Maria is wife)	11 Oct. 1918	L-435
Destruel, Jean; wife	18 Apr. 1905	J-64
Deveraux, Carrie M.; E. W.	27 Aug. 1894	H-96
Devere. Fred A., married	22 Mar. 1867	B-98
Dewey, John A.; Clara	4 Aug. 1909	K-247
Dewey, Wm. H., married	21 Dec. 1896	H-514
DeWolf, Maria E., widow	13 May 1889	F-564
Dibble, Jenie	15 Dec. 1905	J-115
Dickson, John M.; wife	19 Sep. 1895	H-288
Diebold, Regina/Regine; Geo. (I-242)	23 Oct. 1890	G-137
Dies, Jennie B.; Carl M.	24 Dec. 1900	I-310
Dietz, Garhart, insolvent debtor; probate	23 Dec. 1893	F-44
Dillom, C. H.; wife, M. J.	24 Aug. 1868	B-257
Dimauro, Elida; husband, Joseph	2 Jun. 1920	M-37
Dinwiddie, Jas. L., married (G-146)	7 Dec. 1872	B-612
Dittamore, H. A., married	8 Nov. 1877	D-172
Doane, Blanche W.; L. W.	30 Jul. 1907	K-63
Dobner, L.; Annie	11 Mar. 1914	L-65
Dodge, Abiel B.; wife	29 Aug. 1904	J-28

Applicant and Family Information Name	Filing Date	Vol.-Pg.
Dodge, Pardom M., married	8 Feb. 1861	A-131
Dodge, W. R.; wife, Susan G.	22 Dec. 1860	A-82
Dohn, Amelia H.; Geo. E.	1 Sep. 1890	G-107
Dolan, Anne; Peter	23 Jan. 1878	D-208
Donahue, James M.; Ella C.	13 Apr. 1908	K-115
Donahue, Mary J.; Thos. P.	24 Jun. 1895	H-234
Donatella, Antonio, unmarried	13 Aug. 1888	F-486
Dondero, Rosa; John B.	20 Oct. 1891	G-249
Donnelly, John; wife, Bridget (A-575)	8 Oct. 1860	A-34
Donnelly, John; Ann	1 Mar. 1873	B-635
Donnelly, Thomas (Donelly), married	10 Aug. 1872	B-592
Donner, Margaret J., widow	6 Feb. 1886	F-219
Donnohoe, Joann; John	19 Jul. 1883	E-352
Donovan, Laura M.; John M.	5 Jun. 1916	L-281
Dont, Joseph (L-69); Kate	19 Jun. 1876	C-533
Doolittle, T. B.; wife	20 Mar. 1880	D-540
Doran, Wm. M.; Sarah	12 Dec. 1868	B-292
Dorman, Catherine, married	24 Apr. 1876	C-514
Dorman, Jane Wiley; husband, James	16 Sep. 1872	C-121
Dornbach, Frederick J.; Ella F.	6 Aug. 1918	L-423
Dornell, P. A.; wife, (Darnell)	18 May 1897	H-589
Dorwood, Rose T.; Paul A.	5 Sep. 1913	L-29
Dottarar, W. S.; Mary J.	20 Dec. 1916	L-320
Dotter, Cayetono Maria C.; husband, William C.	25 Apr. 1862	A-471
Doty, Susan W.; Willet R.; son Edwin W. by a former wife	26 May 1877	D-132
Doty, Willet R., head of family (same property as D-132)	30 Oct. 1877	D-170
Doud, Philo, married (C-527)	24 Apr. 1876	C-513
Dougherty, Clementia L.;,widow; 2 minor children, (C-194)	8 Sep. 1870	B-446
Dougherty, John, unmarried	9 Jan. 1884	E-418
Dougherty, John; wife	23 Jun. 1898	I-89
Douglas, George W.; Annie M.	2 Dec. 1907	K-82
Dout, Mary; Joseph	12 Jun. 1889	F-578
Dovey, Richard; wife, Jane	23 Apr. 1861	A-270
Dow, Florence H.; husband	20 Jun. 1894	H-64
Dow, Mary, married	5 Jan. 1875	C-363
Dow, Tamar; Wm. B.	11 Dec. 1866	B-60
Dow, Wm. B., widower	28 Dec. 1860	A-87
Dowd, Margaret C.; Henry L.	15 Mar. 1915	L-152
Dowd, Sarah; husband, James E.	12 Nov. 1918	L-447
Dowling, Wm. M.; wife, Margaret	23 Apr. 1861	A-322
Downing, William H., married	3 Feb. 1871	B-490
Dows, Samuel, married	31 Jul. 1873	C-213

Applicant and Family Information Name	Filing Date	Vol.-Pg.
Drago, Margaret T.; Nelson, Sr. (I-340)	25 Oct. 1888	F-513
Draper, J. H.; wife, Elizabeth; probate	26 Feb. 1896	F-390
Dratt, Andrew, married	20 May 1872	C-97
Drever, Harriett; husband, David	2 Jul. 1877	C-564
Driscoll, John; wife	26 Jun. 1880	D-586
Driver, David; Harriet	29 Dec. 1877	D-191
Drosbach, Andrew; wife, Fredricka (Andrew dec'd 4/9/1894; F-97; probate)	1 Aug. 1891	G-211
Drummond, Mrs. Harriet E.; E. W.	8 Nov. 1889	F-617
Dryden, W. R.; wife	10 Sep. 1885	F-128
DuBois, Albertine P.; Joseph C.	4 Feb. 1916	L-252
Ducker, Wm.; wife, Sarah	7 Dec. 1860	A-71
Dufault, Emelia/Emelie, wife of Oliver "Duval"; signature: "Dufautt"	1 Jul. 1886	F-283
Duff, Belle C.; James M. (D-36)	20 Mar. 1876	C-504
Duffy, Thomas; wife, Mary E. (4/19/1889; F-558)	30 Jun. 1879	D-429
Dugan, P. S., married	17 Apr. 1877	D-107
Duhring, Frederick; wife, Dorathea (3/10/1890, D-538; probate)	10 Oct. 1860	A-37
Dumas, Wm.; wife, Sarah	23 Apr. 1861	A-271
Dunbar, John; wife	8 Mar. 1895	H-184
Dunbar, Mrs. Mary; W. A.	1 Aug. 1902	I-408
Dunbar, Wm. F.; wife,	19 May. 1876	D-31
Duncan, A., wife	8 Feb. 1879	D-383
Duncan, John R., married (A-709; B-249; B-571)	31 Mar. 1865	A-646
Duncan, Minnie; C. A.	26 Feb. 1904	J-2
Dunn, Emily; Geo. E.	7 Aug. 1916	L-298
Dunn, Mary; husband, Andreso	2 Jan. 1867	B-65
Dunne, Jno.; wife, Ellen	12 Apr. 1862	A-431
Dunning, Richard W.; Emma	29 May 1908	K-128
Dunwoody, Emaline; husband, A.	23 Dec. 1873	C-269
Durand, Nettie; Ira A.	25 Sep. 1909	K-264
Durst, Ella; John J.	16 Jun. 1916	L-284
Dutard, Leonee Jacques; wife	18 Aug. 1888	F-494
Dutil, Albert Robert; wife, Hilda; 2 minors	3 May 1920	M-29
Dutton, Emily; Reed	27 Apr. 1891	G-187
Dutton, Mary Jane; James R.	11 Feb. 1886	F-224
Dutton, Mary; W. H.	20 May 1890	G-43
Dutton, N. T., Phoebe P. (K-88)	13 May 1902	I-391
Duval, Lucy T., head of family; 2 minors	15 Jul. 1891	G-204

Applicant and Family Information	Filing Date	Vol.-Pg.
Eagleson, Ernest G.; wife	23 Dec. 1897	I-31
Eakin, J. P.; wife	5 Jan. 1891	G-156
Eastman, Peter; wife	1 Jun. 1882	E-225
Eaton, H. H.; Ethel L.	16 Jul. 1915	L-195
Eaton, Isaac; wife, Elizabeth M.	2 Oct. 1867	B-146
Ebeling, H. W.; Minnie	1 Jul. 1909	K-239
Ebers, Abbie A.; H. F.	11 Sep. 1886	F-306
Eby, Aaron; wife, Jennie	7 Oct. 1905	J-99
Eckman, John; wife; 11 children	2 Jan. 1902	I-371
Eckstein, C. W., married; a son	27 Oct. 1910	K-343
Edelmann, Johan/Jakob; wife	10 Aug. 1887	F-400
Edminister, Lucy A.; James L.	19 Dec. 1892	G-386
Edsall, J. B., a widow; 2 minors	19 Nov. 1885	F-165
Edwards, Edward; Sarah	14 Jun. 1878	D-267
Edwards, Edward; Hannah	14 Dec. 1868	B-294
Edwards, H. S.; Susie	2 Aug. 1909	K-245
Edwards, Harry S.; wife	16 Sep. 1908	K-166
Edwards, Herbert H.; Angela G.	13 May 1908	K-124
Edwards, J. C.; widower; 2 daughters	23 Mar. 1916	L-264
Edwards, James; wife	12 Feb. 1880	D-521
Edwards, Johanna; married	25 Sep. 1865	A-673
Edwards, Susie E.; Harry S.; Harry, 7; Angelina, 6; June, 4;	6 Oct. 1913	L-34
Edwards, Uriah; wife, Hannah	19 Apr. 1862	A-448
Egan, Dan; wife, Nellie	23 Nov. 1875	C-458
Egner, Margretha; husband, John	21 Oct. 1875	C-450
Ehrlich, F.; wife, Adolphino	1 Dec. 1868	B-280
Eldridge, Wm; wife, Jane; (A-661); (C-242)	24 Apr. 1861	A-320
Eliason, W. A.; Carrie	9 Aug. 1864	A-614
Ellingwood, Auburn W.; wife, Anna J.; 6 children (L-351)	7 Jun. 1917	L-232
Elliot, Rebecca J.; Wm. R.	10 Feb. 1897	H-532
Elliott, Mrs. Ellen L.; Milton	18 Mar. 1913	K-492
Ellis, Jacob M., married	9 Feb. 1869	B-313
Ellis, Jno. J.; wife, Sarah J. (A-659)	17 Apr. 1861	A-235
Ellis, Margaret S.; John D. (L-183)	2 May 1910	K-315
Ellsworth, Charlotte M.; Legrand	27 Mar. 1889	F-543
Ellyson, Sebe; J. J.	10 Feb. 1897	H-546
Elmore, Sam'l O.; wife, Mary Jane	28 Jul. 1860	A-11
Elmore, Samuel O., married	24 Nov. 1868	B-279

Applicant and Family Information	Filing Date	Vol.-Pg.
Elphick, Edna Roberts; James (L-299)	4 Sep. 1912	K-445
Elphick, Eliza F.; Thomas R.	2 Sep. 1893	G-457
Elphick, Emma M.; Clarence R. (J-17)	12 Nov. 1903	I-484
Elphick, James F.; Hettie (declaration, her name & her signature)	16 Mar. 1885	F-39
Elwell, Clara E. B.; Charles S.	9 Dec. 1889	E-608
Ely, Elisha; wife, Asmath N. (C-384)	24 Apr. 1861	A-302
Emelio, J.; wife	1 Nov. 1886	F-323
Emenegger, Centennia; Frank	1 Feb. 1910	K-292
Emerson, John P., married	11 Jul. 1874	B-656
Engelbert, C. W.; wife	20 Oct. 1890	G-132
Engelhardt, Wilhelmina; John	13 Oct. 1891	G-244
Engelhart, Frederick; wife	1 May 1880	D-562
Engelke, Louis; no wife; 6 minors	29 Aug. 1898	I-112
Engelund, Jorgen P.; wife, Anna D.; no minors	21 May 1919	L-474
England, Eliz. H.; husband, Barton	3 Feb. 1800	D-512
Engler, Mathias, married	21 Apr. 1864	A-602
Engles, Sam'l; Geraldine	6 May 1879	D-408
Enholm, Maybelle; Christian	6 Jul. 1912	K-436
Ennis, Sarah Jane; husband, F. F.	2 Dec. 1878	D-357
Enos, Annie; Morris	11 Dec. 1907	K-86
Enos, Susie T.; John S.	17 Jun. 1890	G-45
Enrietti, Celestina; husband, Antonio	23 Nov. 1906	K-20
Erb, Kate M.; husband, Fred C.	23 May 1919	L-475
Ernest, M. A.; John L.	9 Oct. 1900	I-298
Esmond, Edward M.; wife	31 Jul. 1896	H-469
Espey, Effa; Geo. M.	27 Oct. 1909	K-274
Espy, Geo. T.; Margaret A. Espy	5 Apr. 1862	A-457
Estes, Lois Frances; M. E.	5 Sep. 1908	K-164
Estinghausen, Elmira; W. A.; Ethel May, 3	17 Jan. 1902	I-374
Evans, C. S.; Mary J.	4 Jun. 1894	H-55
Evans, George; wife	16 May 1889	F-565
Everson, Lillie E.; Wallace R.	19 Nov. 1912	K-470
Evey, Anna L.; J. J.	22 Sep. 1894	H-98
Ewell, Peleg D.; Mary M. (B-500, 2/20/1871)	30 Dec. 1862	A-526
Ewing, A. M.; Lottie L.	22 Aug. 1908	K-158
Ewing, Hattie C.; John	10 Jul. 1902	I-403
Exley, Hattie L.; Geo. H.	23 Jun. 1914	L-87

Applicant and Family Information	Filing Date	Vol.-Pg.
Exley, John Thomas; wife	7 Oct. 1892	G-362
Eybel, John A.; wife	17 Mar. 1899	I-224

Applicant and Family Information	Filing Date	Vol.-Pg.
Faber, Chas. F., insolvent debtor	30 Mar. 1891	G-191
Faber, Serena A.; Carles (Charles?)	30 Jun. 1890	G-64
Faber, Serenia Ann, widow; 2 minor grandchildren	16 Oct. 1911	K-393
Faccini, Maria Saitone; John (Flora, Vittoria, Margherita)	12 May 1920	M-32
Faio, Antonio, aka Anton Brown; wife, Frances (Brown) Faio; 4 minor children; probate	23 Feb. 1897	F-515
Fairbanks, Charlotte; Percy	14 Jan. 1892	G-292
Fairbanks, H. T.; & wife	22 Apr. 1861	A-355
Fairchild, O. G.; Ruth M.	2 Dec. 1899	I-227
Fairchild, Ruth C.; Olif. G.	28 Jul. 1909	K-243
Fairgrieve, Barbara J.; John	14 Nov. 1912	K-468
Fairman, Mary E.; Wm. J.	1 Jul. 1911	K-381
Fales, Antonia, married	24 Feb. 1874	C-286
Fanning, Geo. F.; wife	24 Sep. 1885	F-136
Farish, Wm. A., married	6 Jan. 1871	B-487
Farley, Wm. T.; wife	30 Apr. 1888	F-467
Farmer, C. C.; wife	25 Jan. 1896	H-370
Farmer, J. H.; married	21 Apr. 1877	D-111
Farmer, John H., estate of; Susanna S., widow; & Lou	19 Sep. 1803	I-468
Farrar, Geo. B.; Emily K.	12 Mar. 1861	A-141
Farrar, Jane, married	21 Jul. 1873	C-192
Farrell, E. T., married; wife & 1 child; (C-225)	29 Dec. 1873	C-270
Farrell, Ellen	11 Jul. 1885	F-89
Farrer, Anderson L. & wife, Jane (Jane, dec'd 4 Sep. 1897	5 Oct. 1860	A-33
Farrer, Emily K; with family	27 Oct. 1863	A-568
Faught, Jabez; Laurena	20 Apr. 1861	A-278
Faught, Lou. C.; Wm. C.	6 May 1893	G-418
Faught, Willis; wife, Nancy E. (D-580)	20 Apr. 1861	A-281
Faught, Wm.; Nancy	22 Apr. 1861	A-334
Faure, Frank C.; Mary Elizabeth	28 Jul. 1919	L-487
Favour, Jane; John J.	2 Sep. 1882	E-258
Fay, Hiram	1 Mar. 1898	I-60
Fay, Wilbert L.; Luceba C.	29 Jan. 1907	K-30
Faylor, Minnie; Orson C.	21 Jan. 1899	I-163
Fechtelkotter, Hattie; husband, Henry F.; 2 children	7 Dec. 1905	J-112
Feese, Joseph; Catherine	12 Apr. 1862	A-432
Feliz, Ada B.; Sisto J.	18 May 1915	L-174
Fell, Erastus; wife, Lucy Fell (26 Feb. 1877 D-89)	6 Oct. 1866	B-29

Applicant and Family Information	Filing Date	Vol.-Pg.
Felt, Cecilia; Wm. W.	31 May 1906	K-323
Feltz, M. T.; husband, F. C.	17 Apr. 1919	L-470
Fenger, John; wife	29 Jan. 1863	A-536
Fenno, Anna; Allen	23 Feb. 1916	L-255
Fenno, James E.; wife, Mary E. Fenno	1 Feb. 1861	A-116
Fernald, Johnson; wife, Elizabeth	5 Mar. 1861	A-157
Fernald, Mary Lillian; Johnson (another marriage?)	24 Jan. 1887	E-577
Fernbach, Charles; wife	6 Apr. 1903	I-445
Fernlund, Emanuel; wife	6 May 1904	J-14
Ferrari, Rosie; John	10 Dec. 1906	K-21
Ferreira, Barbara; Manuel F.	21 Mar. 1903	I-435
Ferris, Ida M.; John M.	8 Jul. 1890	G-73
Fetter, Benjamin M., married; Adrianna W. (B-628)	20 Apr. 1861	A-286
Fewell, Jas. M., married	14 Apr. 1868	B-221
Fick, Margaretta F.; John F.	19 May 1887	F-393
Field, Harriet R.; married (5 Feb. 1894, H-24)	14 May 1873	C-157
Field, J. C. & wife; C. E. Field	11 Jan. 1870	B-375
Fields, Mary L.; Thos. W.	26 May 1897	H-593
Fike, Nathan; married (B-54; 27 Sep. 1871 C-20)	25 Dec. 1860	A-84
Filcher, J. T., married	15 Dec. 1877	D-184
Finch, H. P.; wife A. C. (D-134)	28 Apr. 1875	C-390
Finchley, Cecilia A.; Thomas L.	24 Apr. 1861	A-332
Fine, A.; wife	29 May 1879	D-418
Fine, Joff.; wife; (E-463; I-230)	16 Dec. 1882	E-291
Fine, Wood; wife	1 Feb. 1896	H-382
Finerty, Mary; Thos.	19 Aug. 1913	L-24
Finigan, Peter; wife, Joanna (A-16 also)	10 Aug. 1860	A-15
Finlaw, Anna L., widow of Wm.	11 Dec. 1905	J-114
Finley, Abbie Jane, married	21 Dec. 1875	C-468
Finley, Carrie A.; Jefferson D.	8 Oct. 1912	K-458
Finley, J. J.; wife	23 Jun. 1886	F-275
Finley, Joseph J.; married	26 Feb. 1872	C-50
Firebaugh, Charlie Ann, married	2 Jan. 1871	B-481
Firebaugh, H. C.; wife; 2 children	12 Mar. 1873	C-128
Fisher, Augustus, married	13 Apr. 1877	D-105
Fisher, Ed; wife, Anabella (a widow, 19 Feb. 1867, B-85;	18 Apr. 1861	A-246
Fisher, Lizzie E.; Samuel	13 Nov. 1897	I-18
Fisher, Susie; S. C.	10 Sep. 1892	G-345

Applicant and Family Information	Filing Date	Vol.-Pg.
Fisk, Mary M., widow; minor son, Arthur M.	4 Mar. 1909	K-211
Fisk, Rufus; Meribah	23 Sep. 1867	B-150
Fitch, Carrie; Charles	12 Mar. 1900	I-253
Fitch, John B.; with family (4 Apr. 1866 B-7)	20 Sep. 1865	A-672
Fitch, Joseph; Sarah Jane	7 Jul. 1909	K-240
Fitch, Joseph; Mary C.	4 Nov. 1865	A-682
Fitch, Lydia I.; husband, J. B.	11 Nov. 1867	B-161
Fitch, William; Clara Pina (B-514)	1 Apr. 1861	A-183
Fitch, Wm., married	24 Dec. 1872	D-16
Fitzgerald, Richard; wife	13 Oct. 1893	H-3
Fix, J. K.; wife	18 Mar. 1886	F-242
Flanary, Wm. E.; Ann	2 Nov. 1863	A-570
Flannagan, Jennie; John	18 Sep. 1886	F-312
Fleckner, Olivia L.; husband, O. P.	28 May 1920	M-34
Flege, Mary Ann; husband, Henry committed State Hosp. 1867; 2 minor children	22 Jun. 1867	B-123
Flegel, Henry; wife, Mary Ann	13 Dec. 1860	A-78
Fleming, Cecilia; husband, William (17 Apr. 1862, A-439)	18 Apr. 1861	A-249
Fletcher, Berna; husband	7 Mar. 1914	L-64
Fletcher, Duncan; Sarah	19 Oct. 1877	D-166
Flewwelling, C.; wife	24 Oct. 1898	I-137
Flockhart, Gertrude; John	16 Dec. 1918	L-448
Florence, Luanna J.; Marshall	12 Dec. 1893	G-482
Florence, Sylvester C.; wife, Jane B.	10 Apr. 1861	A-212
Florence, Vieva M.; Arthur	1 Mar. 1901	I-318
Flynn, Henry, married	7 Oct. 1875	C-442
Fochetti, Julius; widowed dau.; unmarried dau.; 2 minor grandchildren	3 Oct. 1918	L-432
Foerstler, Mary E.; Carl (28 May 1913, L-1; K-389; L-220)	27 Feb. 1903	I-433
Folk, Agnes; James	13 Feb. 1917	L-333
Folks, Jno.; family consists of children only	12 Aug. 1884	E-494
Folks, John, married	2 Jan. 1874	C-241
Ford, Mary E.; husband, W. A. (Mary was formerly Campbell)	2 Jun. 1920	M-36
Foreman, Carl; Gipsy L.	29 Jun. 1916	L-288
Forester, Annie, unmarried; & "my child"	27 Mar. 1876	C-506
Foresti, Frank V., Maria	23 Oct. 1908	K-175
Formschlag, Eliz.; Peter (court order for widow protection)	23 Feb. 1884	E-454
Forni, Gigia; Natale	10 Dec. 1907	K-85
Forrester, A. J.; wife, C. C. Hooper	26 Jun. 1867	B-114

Applicant and Family Information	Filing Date	Vol.-Pg.
Fortson, John T.; Mary Ann (3 Jun. 1874, C-309)	18 Apr. 1861	A-244
Foss, Clark; wife, Lydia Ann	14 Jul. 1866	B-30
Foster, John W.; Nellie A.	9 Jul. 1919	L-485
Foster, Mary Libby; husband, A. B.	1 Dec. 1920	M-62
Foster, Nellie A.; John W.	6 Jan. 1916	L-249
Fouts, Alvin Roy; Amanda O.	9 Oct. 1918	L-433
Fowler, Charlette E.; husband, James E.	9 May 1873	C-132
Fowler, Laura, hd. of household; children of deceased brother	16 Apr. 1881	E-88
Fowler, Minnie A.; N. R.	20 Nov. 1916	L-312
Fowler, Robert F.; wife, M. S.; 9 children; (6/23/1874, C-317; 4/19/1878, C-597)	17 Apr. 1861	A-237
Fowler, Susan A.; James H.	25 Nov. 1882	E-288
Fowler, Warren C.; Jennie; minors Clinton, Doris, Warren, Charlotte	14 Sep. 1912	K-448
Frahm, Margaret M.; John A. H.	11 Feb. 1913	K-487
Frain, Maria T.; husband; (I-356)	1 May 1897	H-584
Frame, Eliza J.; David	18 Apr. 1878	D-250
Franchetti, Mary; Luigi	1 Aug. 1913	L-18
Frank, Hans Ebsen, widower	4 Aug. 1902	I-410
Franklin, D. B.; Winnie	9 Nov. 1883	E-400
Franklin, J. W.; Frances (G-175)	9 Nov. 1887	F-427
Franklin, Wm. F.; wife	7 Apr. 1862	A-419
Franklyn, Winifred; widow; 4 children	18 Jun. 1890	G-57
Fraser, Geo. W.; wife	18 Nov. 1891	G-269
Fraser, Thomas; wife, Julia M.	1 Dec. 1866	B-68
Frasier, Malcom J.; wife	30 Apr. 1887	F-399
Frates, John; wife	3 Feb. 1897	H-530
Frati, Aliessendro; Concetta	22 Mar. 1912	K-419
Frati; Zita; Dominico	9 Jan 1899	I-161
Frazier, Alex. H.; wife	9 Mar. 1880	D-537
Frederichs, Francisco; husband, Gerhard; probate	15 Jun. 1896	F-435
Frederickson, Anna A.; Thorwald	8 May 1915	L-171
Fredrichs, Francisco; Gerhard	18 Aug. 1891	G-219
Fredrick, J. C.; Andine Theodore, wife; minor Alma Louise	8 Jun. 1911	K-380
Freeman, Geo. W., married	26 Sep. 1870	B-453
Freese, Rosa B.; John Herman	6 Apr. 1915	L-159
Freisinn, O. L.; Margarete	24 Aug. 1915	L-208
Freitas, Tony; Isabella	27 Oct. 1914	L-108
French, Eva J.; Chas. F.	19 Mar. 1890	G-28

Applicant and Family Information	Filing Date	Vol.-Pg.
French, Mary Etta; John N.	24 Jul. 1886	F-290
Frese, Rosa B.; John H.	16 Nov. 1901	I-364
Frick, Geo. W.; wife, Mary E. (C-44)	4 Dec. 1869	B-369
Fried, Henry; wife	4 Sep. 1885	F-121
Fritsch, John; wife, C. Soloma	15 Apr. 1861	A-221
Froom, Thornton H., married	9 Dec. 1872	B-615
Frost, Charles; wife	13 Mar. 1884	E-449
Frost, Mary Elizabeth; Harvey Chester	17 Jun. 1919	L-481
Frugoli, Millicent R.; A. J.	7 Mar. 1917	L-337
Fullagar, Caroline, unmarried	27 Sep. 1906	K-2
Fuller, C. E.; wife	17 Feb. 1880	D-524
Fuller, Delia; James P.	5 Jul. 1882	E-238
Fuller, Isaac; Martha; (Isaac single 10 July 1878; D-292)	20 Apr. 1861	A-253
Fuller, Laura W.; Geo. E.	19 May 1890	G-41
Furbee, Katie; Thomas J.	24 Feb. 1890	G-13
Furber, Katie; T. J.	5 Dec. 1891	G-279
Fyfe, Julia C.; mother of minor children	11 Jul. 1885	F-91
Fyfe, William; Jane	31 May 1907	K-47

Applicant and Family Information	Filing Date	Vol.-Pg.
Gaberel, Mattie; Geo. W.; (E-411)	24 Sep. 1881	E-138
Gaggini, Fortunata; Cormelo	3 Sep. 1907	K-72
Gaines, Tabitha Jane; Wm. Crocket	21 Dec. 1881	E-173
Gale, Carrie E.; D. R.	28 June 1900	I-277
Gale, Margaret S.; Cecil H.	29 Apr. 1915	L-168
Gale, Mary L.; Lester L.	5 Apr. 1909	K-228
Gale, Otis S., married	21 May 1874	B-647
Gallagher, John; Margaret	27 June 1863	A-557
Gallandett, James H.; wife	27 July 1882	E-248
Gallard, Catherine; Nicholas	7 Nov. 1895	H-311
Gallo, Rosa Zamorina; Lorenzo	5 Nov. 1889	F-614
Gamble, Aaron W.; wife	1 Aug. 1879	D-444
Gamble, Marie E.; Geo. H.	12 July 1890	G-77
Gammon, Geo. P.; wife	28 Sep. 1878	D-333
Gamsjager, Josef; unmarried (Goemsjoergner, Yosef); no children	11 Feb. 1897	H-542
Ganazzi, Annie A., married	5 Apr. 1878	D-247
Gardella, Catherine; C. L. (her mark as "Caterina")	29 July 1885	F-105
Gardiner, Philip W.; wife	19 Sep. 1903	I-469
Gardner, Cornelia H.; Leonard B.	13 July 1893	G-435
Garrison, Wm.; wife, Mary Jane; (K-221)	20 Sep. 1892	G-347
Garver, Emma A.; James L.; 3 minor children; (K-40)	13 June 1904	J-20
Gaskill, Courtland; wife	26 Aug. 1879	D-457
Gaston, Judson A., married	27 Oct. 1860	A-49
Gater, James E.; wife	22 May 1900	I-274
Gates, Erastus H.; wife, Hattie M.	21 Feb. 1876	C-501
Gates, Rudolph O.	14 July 1904	J-22
Gauldin, Isabell; Josiah, dec'd; (I-11)	31 Jan. 1910	K-291
Gavin, William; Margaret M.	10 Sep. 1909	K-258
Geary, Janet McN.; Thos. J.; (E-555 and abandonments)	23 Dec. 1898	I-159
Gebauers, Auguste; Chas.	1 Aug. 1891	G-209
Gedney, James E.; wife, Emma H.	13 Mar. 1861	A-139
Geer, Cyrus V.; wife, Jennie (Cyrus dec'd 25 May 1889, D-485; probate)	23 Mar. 1887	F-378
Geisselmann, Albert; Helene (K-185)	7 July 1902	I-401
Gemmer, John C.; wife	11 Aug. 1882	E-253
Gentry, Ivy M.; John	8 Feb. 1917	L-331
Gentry, W. O.; E. L., wife (A-643; C-189)	2 Jan. 1864	A-608
Gerard, Eliz.; Emerald, husband	27 July 1878	D-300

Applicant and Family Information	Filing Date	Vol.-Pg.
Gerhardt, Dietz; wife	12 Jan. 1883	E-305
Gerkhardt, H. F.; Christianna	22 Apr. 1862	A-451
Germone, Margherita; G.	6 June 1914	L-83
Getchell, Otis; married	9 June 1873	C-170
Gianotti, Maria, widow; 2 minor children & mother	2 Aug. 1907	K-65
Giauque, Eliz.	5 Feb. 1904	I-495
Gibbens, Margaret M.; R. L.	20 Aug. 1903	I-462
Giberson, Katherine L.; John K.	21 June 1917	L-355
Gibney, Martha C.; Geo.	31 Aug. 1881	E-133
Gibson, Anna Eliza; husband, John (E-357; probate)	18 Apr. 1872	C-89
Gibson, Cordelia J.; James	18 Sep. 1897	H-631
Gibson, Lucena B.; married	27 Sep. 1883	E-382
Gibson, Samira; John R.	9 May 1881	E-93
Gibson, Sarah W.; Henry	10 Nov. 1885	F-161
Gilbert, Jane A.; Jacob	3 Oct. 1863	A-566
Gilbert, Nathan C.; married	28 Apr. 1871	B-515
Gilbert, Platt B.; wife	22 Mar. 1886	F-245
Gilbert, Thomas A., married	11 Dec. 1876	D-58
Gilder, Gertrude; Alfred	24 Aug. 1917	L-365
Gildersleeve, Eliz. R.; Geo. W.	18 Apr. 1903	I-449
Gilham, David T.; married	11 Jul. 1877	C-571
Gillan, Edward; wife, Sarah (Sarah dec'd Nov. 1906; K-19)	24 Apr. 1861	A-339
Gilliam, Lillie M.; S. J.	2 Feb. 1915	L-139
Gilman, Rebecca C.; F. W.	25 Apr. 1916	L-272
Gilmore, R. F.; Eliza or Elizabeth (B-434)	22 June 1865	A-655
Gimberta, Antonia; husband, Andrew	16 Apr. 1919	L-468
Giovanetti, Katie; Domenico	2 Oct. 1917	L-372
Girelli, Peter; Mary; children: Lino, Silvio	3 July 1916	L-290
Gisel, Katrinnes, wife of Jacob	18 June 1889	F-588
Givens, Elisha, widower	17 Sep. 1862	A-505
Givlin, Mrs. Margaret; John (C-121)	21 Oct. 1889	E-602
Gladden, Mary C.; W. N.	21 July 1880	D-595
Glass, Margaret (Marguerite); Philip (H-587)	2 June 1881	E-99
Gleason, Margaret; P. H. (E-591)	7 July 1883	E-350
Glenn, Matilda Jane; Robert	19 Dec. 1887	F-438
Gloeckner, Tamar; Chas.	7 July 1914	L-89
Glynn, F. B., married (H-331)	28 Oct. 1874	C-337
Glynn, Mary J.; Frank	26 June 1890	G-59

Applicant and Family Information	Filing Date	Vol.-Pg.
Gobbi, Marie Louise; Julius	21 Apr. 1915	L-166
Gober, James W.; mother, Rebecca E., widow	16 Aug. 1887	F-405
Gochnauer, Florence A.; Phillip L.	21 Jan. 1898	I-47
Godfrey, T. J., married	17 Mar. 1871	B-497
Goethe, Barbara E.	14 Apr. 1905	J-63
Goetjen, Henry; wife	10 June 1890	G-48
Goetzelmann, Ida; Geo. A.	21 Mar. 1893	G-396
Goldstein, Henry, head of family	4 Apr. 1879	D-395
Goldstein, Sophie, widow; minor child, Isadore	21 Jan. 1898	I-45
Goldstone, Harries; wife	3 Aug. 1864	A-612
Gonsalves, Mary; Frank; dau. Marguerite, 16 yr.	3 Oct. 1913	L-33
Good, Walter C.; Jeanne S.; (Walter dec'd 22 Aug. 1900); probate	2 Nov. 1900	G-508
Goodin, Benjamin F., married (C-8)	26 Apr. 1861	A-351
Goodman, Nellie M.; James Willis; minor son	9 Aug. 1905	J-92
Goodrich, Martha S.; C. B.	10 Feb. 1891	G-168
Goodrich, Sadie; W. D.	17 Oct. 1895	H-302
Goodspead, Anson, married	17 May 1876	D-28
Goodwin, Maria; Enoch	2 June 1882	E-228
Gordon, A. J., married	8 Sep. 1868	B-262
Gore, Gertrude L.; R. F.	2 Feb. 1909	K-204
Gorski, Della Z.; Carl	11 May 1914	L-78
Goshen Eliz.; M. D.	22 Nov. 1898	I-149
Gotzach, Ida A.; Albert H.	30 Dec. 1907	K-89
Gow, A. W.; Edna Blanche	3 Nov. 1913	L-40
Graeff, Clara A., unmarried; has father to maintain	22 July 1911	K-382
Graeter, Henry; wife	15 May 1885	F-52
Graham, Anthony; wife, Ellen (A-630)	29 Oct. 1864	A-623
Graham, Augusta A.; Samuel	30 June 1913	L-10
Graham, Emma; A. R.	3 Feb. 1919	L-461
Graham, James R.; Ann (A-145)	21 Jan. 1861	A-97
Graham, Jennie A.; S. F.	25 Nov. 1912	K-471
Graham, Mary Josephine; Anthony Daniel	4 Dec. 1908	K-191
Graham, Thos. J.; Eleanor Graham	25 Apr. 1861	A-335
Graham, Villa A.; James W. (F-447)	29 Sep. 1883	E-388
Graham, Will Hicks; wife; (A-488)	23 July 1861	A-374
Granger, Matilda; wife of Samuel	6 Sep. 1889	F-606
Granice, Grace I., widow; Harry Hale, dec'd 1/2/1915; children: Celeste, wife of W. P. Murphy; Julia, wife of Dr.	16 June 1915	L-185

Applicant and Family Information	Filing Date	Vol.-Pg.
Fred Sprague; Ramona, wife of Ernest Lynch		
Grant, John D.; Anita F.; (Anita, hd. of family; 1 minor; 12/9/1895, H-336)	4 Apr. 1881	E-84
Grant, Lavina (formerly McCappin); Francis E.	8 June 1916	L-282
Grasso, Mrs. Mary; Womenico	18 June 1901	I-337
Graves, G. W.; wife	28 July 1885	F-103
Graves, Sarah N.; W. S.	9 Dec. 1899	I-232
Gray, Bessie Mrs.; Geo. H.	27 Jan. 1919	L-458
Gray, Eliese	5 Nov. 1920	M-56
Gray, Flora; E. A.	14 Oct. 1918	L-436
Gray, Garett M., wife, Lydia Jane	21 June 1870	B-422
Gray, George B.	3 Apr. 1920	M-27
Gray, Henry Chas.; Lily Haskins, wife	9 June 1902	I-394
Gray, Isaac; Clarissa	27 July 1908	K-147
Gray, Isaac; wife	29 Apr. 1885	F-47
Gray, J. W.; wife, Lillian; 2 children; (K-213)	31 July 1907	K-64
Gray, Nicholas; wife, Ellen N.	26 Apr. 1862	A-484
Gray, Olive; O. L. (L-418)	28 July 1916	L-296
Greaver, John, married	9 Mar. 1869	B-318
Green, C. F., married	10 Oct. 1865	A-681
Green, Fannie S.; Geo.	15 July 1896	H-452
Green, Frank J.; Lillian L.	16 Oct. 1912	K-461
Green, Manuel, Sr.; wife	9 Apr. 1897	H-569
Green, Manuel; wife	31 Jan. 1880	D-510
Green, Marmaduke, widower	4 Sep. 1878	D-317
Greene, Maggie; Samuel T.	29 Dec. 1913	L-52
Greene, Mary E.; Wm.A.	16 Sep. 1909	K-262
Greene, Shadrach; married (C-488)	22 Apr. 1872	C-83
Greenlee, P. M.; wife, Elizabeth	10 Nov. 1866	B-77
Greenwood, Henry; married	15 July 1872	C-113
Greenwood, Mary J.; M. V.	24 Oct. 1900	I-300
Gregoire, Louis; wife, Celestine (Celestine dec'd 11/20/1900, G-519; probate)	12 July 1900	I-278
Gregory, Carolina; James R.	20 Aug. 1900	I-284
Greiner, Frederick (no mention of family)	8 Dec. 1897	I-23
Greiner, Mary L.; Frederick	24 Mar. 1896	H-394
Greist, Eliza; Peter	2 July 1890	G-66
Griess, Catherine; George	4 May 1880	D-564
Griest, Peter; wife, Leah Agnes	15 Apr. 1861	A-227

Applicant and Family Information	Filing Date	Vol.-Pg.
Griffin, Mary E.; Wm.	16 July 1896	H-455
Griffin, Minnie L.; Henry E.	16 July 1896	H-457
Griffin, Patrick, widower	8 Dec. 1894	H-124
Griffith, Annie; S. N.	25 Nov. 1885	F-170
Griffith, Ethelbert E.	22 Jan. 1921	M-70
Griffith, Frederick A.; wife	12 May 1899	I-204
Griffith, Hannah M.; H. C.	8 May 1894	H-47
Griffith, J. A.; probate; (note: probate book B lost)	16 July 1869	B-42
Griffith, James A.; wife, Artamesia	11 Feb. 1865	A-637
Griffitts, Jane Blanche; Edwin Swively	9 Apr. 1914	L-72
Griggs, Joseph H.; Elvenia	3 Apr. 1862	A-423
Grimm, Jeannie M.; widow of Albert; minors Dorothy, Kenneth (notarization: "Est. of Frederick Grimm, dec'd")	23 May 1917	L-349
Grimmer, Chas. A.; Martha K.	28 Oct. 1901	I-359
Grindle, Monroe W.; Mary H.	7 Dec. 1914	L-121
Griswold, May	3 Apr. 1920	M-27
Grove, Catharine, married	20 Apr. 1876	C-512
Groves, Christian C.; J. W.	29 Apr. 1864	A-605
Gruidl, Joseph, Antonette	29 Mar. 1918	L-404
Grundy, Mary Jane, married	31 Mar. 1873	C-139
Gruwell, R. M., married	20 Jan. 1876	C-479
Gryff, John A.; Magdalina (John dec'd 5/16/1898, G-160; probate)	11 June 1866	B-314
Guerin, Ellen; James P.	4 Mar. 1897	H-550
Guidotti, Teresa; Francisco	6 Jan. 1900	I-238
Guilfoyle, Mary; Patrick	28 May 1880	D-579
Guinan, Sarah; James	26 Nov. 1912	K-473
Gully, Elsie M.; Frank J.	11 Jan. 1908	K-92
Gum, Isaac; Clara; 4 children; (Isaac dec'd 3/19/1894, F-82; probate)	31 Dec. 1888	F-526
Gunning, Wm. C.; Anna	6 June 1873	C-167

Applicant and Family Information	Filing Date	Vol.-Pg.
Haefke, Augusta, widow	2 Nov. 1897	I-9
Hagan, Mary; Henry	19 Aug. 1876	C-547
Hagemann, Judith E.; Victro	12 Aug. 1872	B-588
Hagmayer, Beatrice; Gotlieb	3 Mar. 1890	G-22
Haigh, Emma; Edwin	12 Aug. 1901	I-347
Hakes, Rebecca; Door	30 Aug. 1872	B-597
Hale, M. N.; Mary J.	26 Oct. 1889	F-609
Hall, Agnes; Charles H.	12 Aug. 1902	I-409
Hall, Albert A.; wife	18 July 1881	E-116
Hall, Amos T.; wife	5 May 1886	F-253
Hall, David W.; married	11 Dec. 1880	E-54
Hall, Lowry B.; married; (2/28/1880; E-11, E-55)	27 Oct. 1873	C-251
Hall, Mary Ann; husband; 3 children; (8/19/1876, C-548)	4 Sep. 1873	C-218
Hall, Mildred Eunice; George David Hall, husband	24 Sep. 1914	L-105
Hall, Nellie C.; John H.	4 Oct. 1898	I-129
Hall, Robert K., married	22 May 1877	D-130
Hall, Sarah D.; M. V.	10 Mar. 1879	D-387
Halloran, Edward; Duranda	8 Jan. 1876	C-477
Halloran, Mary, married	25 May 1875	C-404
Hamilton, Geo. W.; wife	20 Feb. 1899	I-183
Hamilton, Harriet; Guy S.	2 Oct. 1886	E-569
Hamilton, Mida M.; William J.	26 Aug. 1915	L-209
Hamlin, Carmen A.; Roscoe E.	20 Aug. 1919	L-490
Hamm, William, married	29 Jun. 1874	C-318
Hammell, Henry H.; Leurnia	18 Aug. 1879	D-452
Hammer, M. B.; Mary	5 Sep. 1860	A-28
Hampton, Clara E.; Herbert H.	26 Feb. 1915	L-147
Haney, Ella J.; Frank	24 Dec. 1886	F-349
Hanford, Mary E.; Edwin D., Sr.	21 Nov. 1911	K-403
Hanna, James G.; Mary P.; (F-523)	10 May 1880	D-568
Hannan, Patrick, married	11 May 1877	D-123
Hansen, Christian; wife; (9/12/1902, I-414)	28 Oct. 1885	F-148
Hansen, John Peter; wife	12 June 1901	I-336
Hansen, Louisa; aka Jones, widow	30 July 1918	L-421
Hansen, Margaret; Wm.	26 Aug. 1909	K-252
Hansen, Pauline W.; husband, Henry W.	11 May 1917	L-347
Hanson, Ellen, married	24 Apr. 1869	B-327
Hanson, Jennie A.; E. P.; (F-358)	16 Dec. 1886	F-336

Applicant and Family Information	Filing Date	Vol.-Pg.
Hanson, Mary; Ole	24 Aug. 1896	H-473
Hanson, Nettie P.; John F.	12 May 1915	L-173
Hanson, Wm.; wife	5 June 1888	F-472
Haratzthy, Agostan; Elenor (Abandonments)	18 Jan. 1861	A-107
Harbin, Leander (Harbine); married	27 Nov. 1867	B-169
Harden, Parley, widower	8 Oct. 1883	E-390
Hardesty, Clarinda Ann; Charles W. (F-415)	24 Mar. 1887	F-376
Hardin, Bridget F.; William (E-417; E-508)	15 Feb. 1882	E-193
Hardin, Clara E.; William G.	20 Oct. 1916	L-309
Hardin, J. A.; Agnes	18 Feb. 1861	A-119
Harding, Edwin H.; family	29 Oct. 1883	E-397
Harding, Ellen; widow of Wm. A.	31 Jan. 1895	H-152
Hardt, H. W.; wife; (G-82; L-153; F-449)	23 June 1887	F-397
Hardy, Olive H.; Jonathan	13 June 1903	I-455
Harman, L. N.; Martha	18 Apr. 1861	A-297
Harmer, Will L.; wife, M. Effie; children: Lillian, Clara, Margaret	17 Dec. 1913	L-48
Harmon, Elizzie; F. V.	3 Nov. 1885	F-157
Harney, Sarah; John H.	7 Apr. 1893	G-409
Harper, Evilina M., married	20 May 1874	B-646
Harrington, May; husband, Frank W. (daughter, Clara L.)	24 Jan. 1917	L-326
Harris, E. D.; Maud E.; 3 children; (L-4)	23 Sep. 1893	G-464
Harris, George, married	26 Apr. 1861	A-357
Harris, Jacob; Phebe	17 Dec. 1863	A-577
Harris, M. A.; T. M., husband	5 Nov. 1891	G-261
Harris, Mary E.; R. A.; (J-18; H-629)	27 Sep. 1892	G-351
Harris, Mrs. Hattie; J. W.	29 Mar. 1887	F-380
Harris, Phebe; Jacob ;(G-257)	15 Dec. 1876	D-60
Harris, Sarah E.; Sidney E.	19 Mar. 1861	A-170
Harris, Thomas S.; wife	31 Dec. 1885	F-189
Harris, Zela Zoe; James Wm.; son, Orin H., 8 yrs.	17 Dec. 1918	L-469
Harrison, G. R.; Alice V.	6 Dec. 1910	K-352
Harrison R., married	9 Aug. 1870	B-441
Harrison, Wm. H., married	5 Dec. 1868	B-288
Hart, Amelia Allen; Emmett	26 Aug. 1909	K-253
Hart, Frankie; husband, R. C.	30 Aug. 1895	H-270
Hart, Louisa M.; Henry H.	15 June 1861	A-371
Hart, Marion, wife	9 Nov. 1904	J-44

Applicant and Family Information	Filing Date	Vol.-Pg.
Hart, Phoebe; Emmet; (12/20/1904, abandonment B-20)	8 Oct. 1902	I-413
Harter, Bloomfield; wife Mary I.	10 Nov. 1875	C-454
Hartman, Hattie; William D.	21 Jan. 1887	E-574
Hartzell, J. W.; wife	25 July 1892	G-329
Harvey, L. B., married	20 Feb. 1873	B-633
Harvey, R. A., married	14 Nov. 1876	D-54
Hasek, Karla; Frank J.	8 Jan. 1917	L-324
Haskell, Barnabus; Abigail A.; (3/26/1874 C-298)	12 Apr. 1861	A-347
Haskell, Charles; wife	5 Apr. 1892	G-311
Haskell, Wm. H.; Abbie J.	26 Dec. 1868	B-305
Haskins, Robt.; wife	20 Jan. 1888	F-451
Haskins, T. J., married	26 May 1874	B-649
Haskins, T. J.; and wife (insolvent debtor: Court record: "Haskins & Caldwell"; (4/2/1888, F-459)	31 Mar. 1888	F-458
Hassett, Ora T.; wife	6 July 1894	H-74
Hassett, Sarah E.; widow; minor grandchild, Nellena Walker	27 May 1898	I-80
Hastings, Emily; F. D.	16 Sep. 1913	L-30
Hastings, Martha A.; Joseph C.	7 Jan. 1915	L-132
Hatch, M. J.; wife	4 June 1887	F-394
Hatfield, James M.; Mary Ellen	21 June 1866	B-2
Hatfield, Marietta; John	14 Apr. 1869	B-325
Hathaway, Harriet N. E.; Jeffrey N.	6 Mar. 1920	M-21
Hausmann, Catherine; Ernest A.	2 July 1884	F-14
Hawkins, Margaret A., widow of Jesse	16 May 1867	B-107
Hawthorne, A. C.; husband, J. G.	27 June, 1896	H-448
Hayden, Catherine P.; husband, E. W.	24 Apr. 1897	H-579
Hayden, Stephen C.; Charlotte	18 Apr. 1862	A-444
Hayes, Annie; John	5 Jan. 1891	G-155
Hayes, Emily M.; J. D.	26 July 1920	M-46
Hayes, Mary, widow	15 July 1882	E-243
Hayne, Julia; Patrick	7 Aug. 1860	A-8
Hays, Mrs. Mary Jane, married	30 Aug. 1866	B-41
Hays, Robert K., married	15 Feb. 1875	C-371
Hayselden, Thomas; wife	20 June 1893	G-428
Hayward, D. L.; Mary; (7/27/1875, D-425; D-376; probate)	16 Dec. 1869	B-370
Hayward, Jonathan B.; Mrs. Dorleski E.	7 May 1889	F-562
Haywood, Robert E., married	18 Mar. 1875	C-376
Hazelton, Edson R.; Mary E.; one child	13 Aug. 1913	L-22

Applicant and Family Information	Filing Date	Vol.-Pg.
Hazen, Frank; Myra F.; (L-348)	22 Nov. 1916	K-315
Headley, Mrs. H. C.	26 Sep. 1895	H-290
Heald, Thomas T., married; (D-272)	18 Aug. 1868	B-255
Healey, Eugene J.; Susan A.; 2 children	21 Mar. 1917	L-340
Heath, Wm. A.; wife	19 June 1883	E-344
Hebbron, James R.; Eleanor Hebbron	25 Apr. 1861	A-315
Heckley, Olive D.; T. B.	4 Mar. 1918	L-398
Hedges, N. M. & wife; L. C. H. Hedges; (8/4/1879 D-446)	5 Dec. 1863	A-578
Hedricks, Sarah Jane; Joseph	19 Aug. 1878	D-309
Heffelfinger, W. J.; Laura J.	19 May 1874	C-399
Heffelfinger, W. J.; Hannah	3 Sep. 1872	B-601
Heffron, A. H.; wife	13 Nov. 1879	D-486
Heffron, Albert; Sarah; (4/22/1872 C-87)	27 Oct. 1869	B-360
Heidt, Jeannie; John Jacob	30 Aug. 1890	G-102
Heintz, August Henry; Hermine; 6 children former marriage; Hermine's 4 children by her former marriage	29 Apr. 1915	L-169
Heisel, Ellen; Paul	28 July 1881	E-118
Heizer, Robert, married; (9/10/1873 C-223)	22 Sep. 1870	B-447
Hellwegen, Pauline; husband, Henry A.	5 Nov. 1891	G-260
Helm, Mary E.; Thos. A.	9 Mar. 1895	H-185
Helman, Minnie; William dec'd abt 10 May 1908	25 Apr. 1910	K-312
Helman, Wm; wife	7 Jan. 1892	G-290
Hemenway, Alice; D. D.	6 Sep. 1901	I-353
Hemminger, Benjamin F.; Carrie Ruth	23 Jan. 1911	K-362
Henderson, Harriet; William	30 Oct. 1874	C-340
Henderson, I. M.	15 Apr. 1902	I-385
Hendley, John; Harriet E. Case Hendley	26 Apr. 1862	A-478
Hendley, Laura A.; W. G.	23 June 1898	I-92
Hendrick, E. W., married; (1/2/1873 B-621)	21 Aug. 1866	B-45
Hendricks, J. M.; wife	13 Oct. 1896	H-489
Hendrix, Susan A.; Edwin U.	24 Feb. 1900	I-250
Henelly, Ellen; Patrick	6 Apr. 1895	H-207
Henley, S. B.; wife	18 Mar. 1899	I-225
Hennessey, David; Johana Hennessey (Harrison)	12 Feb. 1862	A-400
Henninger, Henry; Dora	30 Oct. 1911	K-398
Henretty, Catherine; Patrick (Hanrety)	2 July 1880	E-20
Henry, Cora L.; Isaac B.	1 May 1902	I-388
Henry, James, (insolvent debtor, H-210); (F-274, probate)	3 June 1895	C-556

Applicant and Family Information	Filing Date	Vol.-Pg.
Hereford, John (order setting aside homestead)	9 Feb. 1863	A-540
Hermann, Margaretha B.; Max.	15 Sep. 1910	K-336
Herrington, James, married	24 Aug. 1874	C-322
Herrmann, Barbory; Christopher	13 Sep. 1886	F-308
Hervey, Alice; N. B.	10 Oct. 1879	D-469
Hess, J. M.; Charlotte	4 Nov. 1915	L-225
Hess, Louisa; Frederick	9 May 1876	B-665
Hevel, Christopher; wife	11 June 1917	L-354
Hevel, Persis A.; Elmer L.; (L-382)	18 May 1915	L-179
Heyward, Nettie; Henry	11 Apr. 1910	K-310
Hibbitts, Amilia F., widow of Michael; (G-110; G-382; F-602)	10 Mar. 1887	F-367
Hickey, Frank P.; wife	10 Apr. 1905	J-61
Hickey, Maurice; family	30 Dec. 1882	E-295
Hickey, Nora; Patrick J. C.	27 Dec. 1893	H-13
Hickey, P. F.; wife	16 July 1902	I-405
Hicks, E. S.; wife; (I-438)	18 Oct. 1886	F-317
Hicks, Lucy B.; O. V.	15 Mar. 1915	L-151
Hicks, Moses C.; Elizabeth A.	31 Jan. 1872	C-33
Hiett, Edith, widow of George	17 Apr. 1872	C-75
Higby, W., by order of court (Note: unable to locate in Book F)	3 Feb. 1888	F-451
Higby, Wm; wife	26 Nov. 1881	E-161
Higgins, Mrs. Jennie M.; Henry E.	14 Jan. 1890	E-618
Hill, Eliza R.; George A.	6 Sep. 1878	D-320
Hill, J. H. & wife; (Joseph Henry)	7 Jan. 1896	H-351
Hill, James M., married	12 Apr. 1862	A-430
Hill, Mary B.; Samuel R.	3 Feb. 1910	K-294
Himebauch, Jos.; Maria	1 July 1875	D-23
Hinds, Julia A.; H. B.	26 June 1872	C-110
Hinkle, Arabella, married	3 Apr. 1861	A-201
Hinkston, Mary A. E.; Joseph R.; daughters over 18: Annie, Alice; probate	2 Nov. 1891	E-240
Hirth, Susanna, widow of Frederick	30 May 1903	I-440
Hixson, John; wife; (K-341)	27 Jan. 1903	I-429
Hoag, O. H., married; (D-293)	16 May 1870	B-406
Hoar, Emma Linda; C. A., husband	5 Oct. 1916	L-305
Hoar, Virginia S.; B. F.	16 Mar. 1910	K-304
Hobbie, John; wife	26 Jan. 1899	I-167
Hobbs, Caroline; E. M.	16 June 1885	F-78

Applicant and Family Information	Filing Date	Vol.-Pg.
Hobbs, G. W.; married	23 June 1876	C-535
Hockin, Margaret L.; Wm. H.; (L-322)	20 Jan. 1913	K-484
Hocklin, A. E.; Wm,, husband	2 June 1896	H-431
Hodges, H. C.; wife	26 Mar. 1891	G-180
Hodgkins, Edwin T.; Clora E.	23 Sep. 1912	K-451
Hoen, Berthold; wife; (E-272)	13 Oct. 1882	E-270
Hofeldt, Doris (Dorothea); Emil	8 Aug. 1914	L-94
Hoffer, Augusta; C. A.	28 Sep. 1898	I-124
Hoffer, Christina; Frederick	9 Feb. 1882	E-191
Hoffer, Frederick; Christina	9 Apr. 1883	E-319
Hoffer, Virgil; Gertrude	30 Apr. 1914	L-78
Hoffman, Frederick Wm., married	5 July 1871	B-548
Hogan, Thomas; wife; (E-64)	5 Dec. 1878	D-359
Hogle, Weltha A. G., married	16 Nov. 1871	B-581
Holcomb, Alfred O., head of family	20 Aug. 1914	L-97
Hollenbeck, Anita; J. T.	16 June 1902	I-396
Hollman, Frederick; wife	22 Apr. 1904	J-12
Holloway, Bessie M.; Geo. K.	4 Sep. 1896	H-482
Holloway, Richard; Mary A. (Declaration)	18 Jan. 1861	A-110
Holly, Sidney B.; wife; (1/20/1882 E-183)	23 Oct. 1880	E-40
Holman, John H.; Margaret	26 Apr. 1862	A-473
Holman, Margaret J.; John H.	15 Dec. 1875	C-466
Holman, Nancy A.; widow of Isaac A.	26 Apr. 1862	A-474
Holmes, Albert, married	16 Apr. 1873	B-640
Holmes, Annie M., widow	11 Apr. 1904	J-10
Holmes, Cleta; Calvin	15 Sep. 1919	L-498
Holmes, H. P.; wife	7 Sep. 1888	F-503
Holmes, Katie A.; C. J.	1 June 1920	M-35
Holmes, Lucy; (A-3)	28 Jan. 1863	A-535
Holmes, Ovid; Ruth; 1 child	10 Jan. 1916	L-250
Holmes, Sarah A.; Henry	24 Sep. 1894	H-100
Holt, W. A. S., married; (E-438)	10 Jan. 1878	D-197
Holton, Mary A.; P. H.; (E-533; probate)	27 Sep. 1875	C-439
Honor, Bertha M.; Henry	17 Apr. 1914	L-75
Honsa, Joseph; wife	15 Jan. 1903	I-428
Hood, Carrie E.; Thomas B.	11 July 1881	E-113
Hood, Daisy Dean; Benjamin Henry	23 Dec. 1918	L-451
Hood, John; Florence R.; 4 children	6 Feb. 1917	L-330

Applicant and Family Information	Filing Date	Vol.-Pg.
Hooper, P. J., married	22 Oct. 1866	B-50
Hooton, Jesse; Elizabeth	29 Sep. 1862	A-509
Hopes, Ellen R.; Edward	25 July 1879	D-440
Hopkins, E. G., married	15 Feb. 1873	B-631
Hopkins, Mary; T. J.	23 Apr. 1877	D-118
Hopper, Telitha; Amos H.	23 July 1877	C-579
Hopper, Thomas, Jr.; wife	7 Nov. 1902	I-412
Hopper, Wm.; Talitha	17 Apr. 1861	A-240
Horn, Frank C.; Mathilda; (Year 1919, M-4)	24 June 1912	K-432
Horn, John W.; Louise; 3 children: Herbert, Marjorie, Edith W.	19 Dec. 1917	L-388
Hornbuckle, Thomas J., single	3 Oct. 1888	F-510
Horne, Annie F.	5 Sep. 1894	G-497
Horr, Sarah A.; Riley J.	11 Aug. 1915	L-203
Hottinger, Catherine; husband, B.	2 Apr. 1895	H-204
Hough, Clark A.; Elizabeth Ann	14 Mar. 1861	A-162
Houseley, Jos. W.; wife	25 Sep. 1885	F-138
Howard, Horace A.	27 Mar. 1889	F-544
Howard, S. D., married	29 Jan. 1868	B-198
Howe, Chas. J.; Maude; (G-55)	12 May 1887	F-392
Howe, E. A., married	12 Mar. 1874	C-292
Howe, Louisa; Geo. G. ;(I-355); probate	8 Jan. 1894	F-53
Howe, Maude; Charles J., dec'd; minors: Babe & Howard	15 Dec. 1909	K-282
Howe, Phillip, married	25 Nov. 1871	B-584
Howell, John G.; Annie B.	3 May 1870	B-404
Howell, L. V. H., widower & family	30 Sep. 1870	B-454
Hoyt, Elijah, married	10 July 1866	B-27
Hoyt, Leah Louise; Frank L.	24 June 1912	K-430
Hoyt, Ora M.; Henry Auren	24 June 1912	K-431
Hubbard, Sarah J., married	5 May 1875	C-393
Huber, Emma; Henry	23 June 1914	L-88
Hudson, Ann; Samuel	7 June 1862	A-491
Hudson, Frank W.; Eliza Jane	15 Apr. 1862	A-436
Hudson, Henry W., insolvent debtor; probate	19 Jan. 1892	E-304
Hudson, Mrs. M. E.; Martha & family	4 May 1880	D-563
Hudson, Thomas; Mary Catherine	29 June 1868	A-656
Hughes, Ada C.; Humphrey	8 Dec. 1894	H-123
Hughes, Arthur R.; wife	2 Feb. 1895	H-156

Applicant and Family Information	Filing Date	Vol.-Pg.
Hughes, Ernest J., single	10 May 1882	E-217
Hughes, Hugh; Monica; Christiana Doratha Carolina	20 July 1871	B-531
Hughes, Mary J.	25 Sep. 1894	G-499
Hughes, Mrs. H. J.; (Emma A.); children	21 Mar. 1917	L-340
Huie, Geo. W.; Sallie E.	26 Nov. 1860	A-69
Hulbert, Chas. J., head of family	27 Dec. 1894	H-130
Hulbert, H. Perry; wife	12 Jan. 1895	H-137
Hulbert, Wm.; Lydia; (12/27/1866 B-59)	7 Jan. 1861	A-101
Humphrey, Ora May; Walter S.	6 June 1901	I-334
Humphries, Catharine, married	24 Feb. 1874	C-284
Humphries, Catherine; Charles	23 Oct. 1883	E-393
Humphries, Charles, married; (F-51)	6 July 1875	C-414
Hunnewell, G. A.; wife	3 Nov. 1900	I-301
Hunt, Andrew, married	8 June 1868	B-243
Hunt, Benjamin W.; Elizabeth Y. Sullivan Hunt	28 Aug. 1865	A-668
Hunt, Charles; Sophia; (10/13/1876 D-43; E-304)	14 Dec. 1868	B-296
Hunt, Cora Belle; Paul	26 Nov. 1913	L-42
Hunt, Wm. J., head of family	4 Sep. 1878	D-319
Hunter, John	26 Mar. 1874	C-296
Huntly, G W., divorced; (5/25/1896 H-426)	27 Dec. 1895	H-340
Huntly, Joseph; Keziah	13 Oct. 1869	B-355
Huntoon, Sarah; Philander	20 Mar. 1895	H-196
Hunziker, Jane; G.	13 Dec. 1881	E-170
Hurd, Geo. W.; Cora	30 June 1886	F-281
Hurd, John; Estella	10 July 1901	I-342
Hurlbut, Edwin T. M.; wife	20 June 1881	E-106
Hurlbut, Helen; E. T. M., husband	24 Aug. 1897	H-615
Hurst, Henry J.; Sarah H.	24 Dec. 1913	L-51
Husler, Alvois; wife	6 Dec. 1899	I-228
Husler, E. A.; wife, Dora; Elwin, 19 yrs.; Dorothy, 15 yrs.	6 Jan. 1915	L-131
Hutchings, Mary; Thomas	19 Aug. 1903	I-461
Hutchinson, Elsie May; Samuel J.	22 Jan. 1919	L-456
Hutchinson, Geo. A.; wife	4 Sep. 1900	I-288
Hutchinson, Maude; Lawrence	27 Feb. 1904	J-4
Hutton, Chas. E.; wife, S. E.; (B-675; C-574)	13 Mar. 1872	C-60
Hyde, Patrick; wife	2 Nov. 1888	F-515
Hylton, Deborah R., widow	18 Dec. 1860	A-89
Hylton, Theodore de Marmaduke; Sarah C.	7 July 1862	A-496
Martin, Ella B.; Henry	7 Dec. 1894	H-119

Applicant and Family Information	Filing Date	Vol.-Pg.
Ingalls, Lillie W., widow	4 Jan. 1897	H-518
Ingham, A. H.; insolvent debtor	18 Feb. 1889	F-532
Ingham, Andrew H.; Maria P.	30 Mar. 1909	K-219
Ingram, Fred S.; Thusnelda E.	2 May 1913	K-500
Ingram, Jno.; Wiluna Ann	27 Apr. 1861	A-306
Ingram, Sarah A.; S. D.	15 Oct. 1898	I-134
Isaacs, Sarah A.; Anderson (12/20/1890, G-144)	25 May 1885	F-58
Ivancovich, Nellie R.; Geo. (4/17/1899, I-199)	7 Nov. 1891	G-263
Ivens, C. H.; Mary E.	20 June 1865	A-653
Jacinto, Mary; Joseph	18 Oct. 1900	I-297
Jackman, Elnora J., widow	7 June 1912	K-428
Jackson, Paul; wife	11 May 1903	I-452
Jackson, Solomon, married	28 Apr. 1862	A-486
Jackson, Susan; James L.	2 Jan. 1907	K-28
Jackson, Thos J.; Caroline Johnson (Thos. J. & wife)	20 Oct. 1865	A-676
Jackson, William; Julia Ann (A-703; B-93)	27 Mar. 1865	A-645
Jacobi, Charlotta; Ludwig	2 Nov. 1903	I-482
Jacobs, Alfred S.; married	2 Jan. 1875	C-362
Jacobs, E.; Fanny	13 June 1874	C-313
Jacobs, Mary L.; J. B.	11 Sep. 1882	E-262
Jacobs, Thos. R.; Alzina (E-49)	9 Mar. 1874	C-290
Jacobsen, Mathilde A.; C. A.	7 Oct. 1909	K-269
Jacques, Aurelie; I. F.	12 May 1877	D-125
Jagoe, Mrs. E. M.; R. H.	17 Sep. 1889	E-583
Jameson Etta L.; H. M.	15 Feb. 1885	F-228
Jameson, John C., married	18 Nov. 1870	B-465
Jameson, Samuel E., married	4 Sep. 1877	D-138
Jansen, Fred A.; Adelaide	15 Dec. 1883	E-408
Jansen, J. C.; 2 minors	16 Sep. 1876	C-554
Jarvinen, Alma H.; Frank A.	8 June 1920	M-38
Jason/Hacinto, Mary, head of household, unmarried	29 Dec. 1904	J-48
Jason, May; Joseph (I-401)	26 June 1894	H-67
Jay, David, married	11 Apr. 1878	D-249
Jehle, Sophie; Leo (E-440)	21 Nov. 1879	D-491
Jenkines, J. H.; wife	5 May 1899	I-201
Jenkins, Geo. F., married (C-472)	11 Sep. 1867	B-159
Jenkins, Mrs. Ethel; Henry R.	2 Oct. 1906	K-2
Jenkins, W. L.; Mary E.	2 Mar. 1910	K-301
Jenner, Mary E., married	21 June 1875	C-411

Applicant and Family Information	Filing Date	Vol.-Pg.
Jensen, Ethel M.; F. N.	16 Nov. 1920	M-59
Jeter, W. P., married	16 Aug. 1873	C-203
Jewell, Susan L., single; minor child, abt. 9 yrs.	10 Sep. 1877	D-137
Jewett, George E.; Mary A.	26 Jan. 1863	A-531
Jewett, L. L.; wife	18 Apr. 1892	G-313
Jobbins, Alphaeus; Louisa	30 Apr. 1919	L-471
Johannsen, Edward H.; wife	2 Oct. 1911	K-292
Johnson, Adolph; Ellen	15 May 1867	B-111
Johnson, Adolph; Elsie R.	6 Jan. 1917	L-350
Johnson, Andrew P.; Mary A.	5 May 1910	K-319
Johnson, Clara; Claude Eugene	14 Jan. 1916	L-283
Johnson, Clem A.; Frances F. Box	25 Apr. 1862	A-465
Johnson, Delia A.; David E.	17 June 1902	I-397
Johnson, Emma A.; D. W.; probate	24 Aug. 1896	F-454
Johnson, Farmer; Agnes Jane	16 Jan. 1872	C-30
Johnson, Fred; Mary J. (B-209)	14 Jan. 1864	A-586
Johnson, Geo. W. F.; family	15 Nov. 1882	E-285
Johnson, John Jasper; Polly Ann	4 Nov. 1867	B-165
Johnson, Karen J. (Skaane); estate of Olans J. (Deed Book 246, pg. 465)	18 May 1908	
Johnson, Mamie B.; T. C.	18 Sep. 1907	K-74
Johnson, Mary Alice; Orrick	28 Apr. 1875	C-388
Johnson, Mary; Frank	6 Aug. 1904	J-24
Johnson, Mrs. Mary J., widow (E-469)	20 July 1877	C-578
Johnson, Ole; Christina	23 Jan. 1915	L-137
Johnson, P. E.; S. J., husband	12 Aug. 1878	D-303
Johnson, Robt. F.; Frances L.	9 Dec. 1878	D-360
Johnson, Thos. J.; Caroline (11/25/1863, A-574)	10 Apr. 1862	A-446
Johnson, Wm. M., married	19 May 1871	B-524
Johnston, Alexander; Margaret S. (D-13)	26 Mar. 1870	B-389
Johnston, America A.; John	8 Jan. 1885	F-196
Jones, Charles; Addie	2 Nov. 1908	K-181
Jones, Clarissa J.; Thos. J.; no children; probate	20 Jan. 1888	D-395
Jones, Esma T.; Rosa B., wife	14 Mar. 1910	K-303
Jones, Joseph S.; wife	30 Dec. 1879	D-500
Jones, Louisa, aka Louisa Hansen, widow	30 July 1918	L-421
Jones, Lyman B., married	16 Oct. 1877	D-163
Jones, Margaret E.; Richard	23 Jan. 1895	H-143
Jones, Mary; Thos. B.	9 Nov. 1871	B-579

Applicant and Family Information	Filing Date	Vol.-Pg.
Jones, Mrs. Lavinah B.; Geo. C.	30 Oct. 1883	E-398
Jones, Richard; wife (G-268)	21 Oct. 1891	G-251
Jones, Sydney L.; Ida May	5 Nov. 1917	L-380
Jones, Thos.; Emilia	20 Feb. 1880	D-526
Jones, W. L.; Lizzie Armstrong	3 Mar. 1908	K-105
Jones, Wm. Henry; Rebecca	25 Mar. 1861	A-173
Jordan, Leslie A.; wife	11 Dec. 1902	I-425
Jordan, Mary Jane, married	4 Feb. 1867	B-85
Jordan, Mary Louise; Charles R.	7 Mar. 1910	K-302
Jorgensen, Amalia C.; Charles	26 Dec. 1896	H-516
Jorgensen, Peter C., single, not head of family	21 Apr. 1897	H-575
Jose, Emanuel C.; wife (G-172)	27 July 1888	F-479
Jose, Mary Ann; Michael H.	10 Dec. 1868	B-290
Jose, Michael H.; Mary Ann	21 Feb. 1872	C-47
Joseph, Alfred P.; Hattie	16 Jan. 1909	K-197
Joy, Benjamin; Sarah V. (7/8/1901, I-341)	15 July 1873	C-187
Joy, W. H.; R. A. (9/5/1879, D-458)	19 Jan. 1878	D-204
Julian, John, married	19 Dec. 1877	D-186
Julliard, C. F.; wife (E-374)	22 Jan. 1879	D-380
Justin, Gussie; Frank	8 Nov. 1895	H-313

Applicant and Family Information	Filing Date	Vol.-Pg.
Kadrolavansky, Alexandra, widow of P. J.	18 Mar. 1879	D-388
Kahrs, Alma; L. A.	2 Dec. 1897	I-22
Kalb, Annie M.; Peter J.	28 Aug. 1896	H-478
Karn, Lena R.; John M.	3 Mar. 1913	L-150
Katen, John; wife	11 Mar. 1895	H-187
Kauffmann, Margaret; Charles F. (10/4/1890, G-123)	16 June 1886	F-272
Kavanaugh, Nicholas; Louisa	19 Dec. 1861	A-388
Kean, Serenia Ann; Joseph B.	26 Aug. 1886	F-303
Kearney, Annie; Dennis H. (4/22/1880, D-558)	5 May 1873	C-150
Kearney, Eliz. D.; John	21 July 1880	D-593
Kearns, Mrs. A.; James J.	20 Oct. 1897	I-6
Keaton, Mrs. M. J.; W. M.	4 Feb. 1889	F-531
Keays, Wm. S., married	24 July 1873	C-209
Keeler, Effie B.; John E.	11 Sep. 1906	J-153
Keener, Eleanor; John D.	26 May 1879	D-415
Keim, B. F., no family; probate	9 May 1898	G-147
Keim, Eliza Amanda; R. F. (B. F.?) (2/7/1880, D-518)	4 Jan. 1876	C-474
Keith, Caroline J.; Joseph S.	7 July 1874	B-653
Keller, Esther M.; A. H.	21 July 1920	M-45
Keller, Friedericks; Mary	4 Sep. 1865	A-670
Kelley, Alfred & Eunice	9 Aug. 1880	E-25
Kelley, Jane, widow of W. H.	29 May 1893	G-424
Kelley, John; wife	14 Apr. 1880	D-554
Kelley, Sarah Z.; James	16 Aug. 1888	F-492
Kellogg, Merritt G.; Eleanor K.; one child	16 Nov. 1905	J-109
Kelly, Albert; (Charity G. 10/16/1873; C-247; Charity S. 7/8/1878, D-286)	12 Mar. 1866	A-698
Kelly, Alfred; Eunice H. (1/12/1867, B-79; 6/30/1902; abandonment)	13 Jan. 1866	A-689
Kelly, D. W.; wife; abandonment	13 Dec. 1860	A-77
Kelly, Dan John; Julia	22 Sep. 1862	A-506
Kelly, Daniel W.; Ann	22 Apr. 1861	A-290
Kelly, John, married	24 June 1876	C-536
Kelly, Linnie; Chas. A.	28 June 1904	J-21
Kelly, Margaret; John	11 Dec. 1872	B-616
Kelly, Mary; James W.	7 Aug. 1890	G-84
Kelly, Michael; Norah; no children	17 Sep. 1919	M-2
Kelly, Mrs. Mary; W. P.	6 Mar. 1906	J-123
Kelty, Sarah J.; Geo.	5 June 1871	B-528

Applicant and Family Information	Filing Date	Vol.-Pg.
Kemp, F. B.; Helen B.	2 Apr. 1919	L-466
Kendall, John, married	29 Apr. 1861	A-264
Kenneally, James; Addie; 3 children	2 Feb. 1919	M-20
Kennedy, G. W.; wife	24 Aug. 1886	F-301
Kennedy, Geo. H.; wife	31 Oct. 1887	F-424
Kennedy, Mary; Chas.	16 Sep. 1878	D-325
Kenney, James; Ellen	20 Dec. 1876	D-62
Kenney, Mary; Thomas	1 July 1879	B-680
Kessenich, Henrich, married	2 July 1874	B-651
Kessing, Catherine; Clemens	25 Jan. 1896	H-368
Kettlewell, Mrs. Geo. Wallace	23 May 1896	H-423
Keuerleber, Anna M.; Christ G.	25 Mar. 1913	K-494
Kevany, Michael & Mary	18 July 1878	D-296
Keyes, Barbara; Marshall M., estate, probate	7 July 1890	D-588
Kidd, Abigail W.; widow of Peleg; minor non-resident heirs	12 Sep. 1870	B-449
Kier, Gesa S.; Harry	24 June 1882	E-233
Kill, James, married	17 Feb. 1872	C-45
Killam, P. E.; A. F.	5 July 1889	F-592
Kimball, M. Viola; C. L.	28 Sep. 1893	G-472
Kimball, Majesta; Harrison (Kimble, Kimbel---all 3 spellings shown)	15 Apr. 1889	F-554
Kimble, J. W.; Mary A.	29 Dec. 1879	E-6
Kimes, Cora E.; David M.	16 May 1904	J-16
Kimes, S. C.; wife	24 Apr. 1902	I-386
King, Anna J.; Geo. F.	22 Mar. 1898	I-61
King, John; Anna M.	7 Jan. 1896	H-348
King, Nancy; John T.	17 June 1910	K-325
King, R. A.; Miriam M.	23 May 1885	F-56
King, R. H.; Ann C.	13 Apr. 1861	A-226
King, Robt. A.; wife	27 Oct. 1883	E-395
Kingwell, Benjamin; wife	25 Jan. 1897	H-524
Kinney, Philanda; E. R., husband	18 Apr. 1862	A-442
Kinsman, Annie M.; Richard	11 Nov. 1897	I-20
Kirby, Eliz.; John H.	4 Oct. 1881	E-146
Kirkpatrick, J. S., widower	14 Mar. 1862	A-407
Kirkpatrick, J. M., widower	19 Sep. 1882	E-266
Kizer, Adeline; John Geo. (4/25/1905, J-66)	9 Feb. 1900	I-249
Kizer, Louie P.; Harry J.	28 Apr. 1913	K-498

Applicant and Family Information	Filing Date	Vol.-Pg.
Kizer, Mary E.; Jno. P. (widow 4/23/1877, D-114)	13 Jan. 1871	B-486
Kleiser, James & Lizzie	3 Oct. 1878	D-338
Klieser, Nannie D.; James A.	3 Aug. 1863	A-561
Kloppenburg, C. W., married	10 Dec. 1874	C-352
Klute, Anna C.; Henry (widow 12/31/1884, E-537)	9 May 1882	E-216
Klute, Henry, married	11 Dec. 1874	C-354
Knapp, Mary A., W. L.	7 July 1890	G-71
Knapp, R. I.; Betsy	3 Mar. 1869	B-316
Knapp, Wm. D.; wife	1 Nov. 1894	H-109
Kneller, Geo. W.; wife	10 Mar. 1885	F-32
Knight, Charles S.; wife	24 Dec. 1895	H-338
Knight, Wallace H.; wife	2 July 1894	H-69
Knopp, Frederick, Caroline F.	6 Feb. 1919	L-462
Knox, Jamina; John M. (11/9/1909, K-276; 7/1/1910, K-326)	20 Mar. 1903	I-434
Knox, John H., married	11 Apr. 1870	B-395
Knute, Chas. Louis; wife	18 Nov. 1893	H-6
Kobes, Mary; Chas. B.	5 Aug. 1908	K-150
Koch/Kach, Minnie; August	11 Mar. 1878	D-231
Koch, Mamie I.; Conrad C.	23 Nov. 1910	K-349
Koch, Margaret J.; John	2 June 1898	I-84
Koenig, Mrs. Ellen; Frank (8/1/1881, E-122)	28 Feb. 1889	F-535
Koetitz, Ludie (aka Ludia); Mrs. F. A.; Frederick C. E. A. Administrator; probate	6 Nov. 1904	H-260
Kohle, August; Katrina	31 Jan. 1873	C-126
Kohler, Herman; wife; no children	12 Mar. 1906	J-124
Kohler, Johanna; Wm.	14 July 1915	L-194
Kohnenberger, Katie; Joseph (2/11/1897, H-539)	30 Jan. 1895	H-147
Kopp, Ella H.; John G.	9 Mar. 1908	K-108
Krackert, Marie; Rudolph	31 Aug. 1912	K-444
Kratzer, Janie; D. W.	20 May 1919	L-473
Krausse, J. C. H.; wife	14 Nov. 1889	F-624
Kreichbaum, John George; Lucy	2 Dec. 1868	B-285
Kreuz, Frank P.; Katharina	10 May 1895	H-222
Krom, John, married (Krov or Kron)	24 July 1868	B-253
Kruse, Charles G.; Carrie M.	17 Oct. 1912	K-463
Kruse, Fred; Clara	31 Oct. 1912	K-465
Kruse, Louise J.; Frederick A.	12 Nov. 1908	K-183
Kuffel, Isaac; wife	28 Jan. 1884	E-426

Applicant and Family Information	Filing Date	Vol.-Pg.
Kulberg, Sarah J.; A. J.	22 Aug. 1901	I-351
Kummerle, Emil G.; wife	6 Sep. 1902	I-416
Kykendall, Dollie; James O. (9/18/1906, K-1; 4/24/1916, L-270)	19 Nov. 1895	H-323
Kyle, Thomas; wife	9 Aug. 1894	H-85

Applicant and Family Information	Filing Date	Vol.-Pg.
Label, Heman; Hannah (2/21/1881, E-77)	17 Apr. 1868	B-227
Lafferty, Annie O.; H. C.	21 Apr. 1898	I-67
Lafferty, H. H.; married	7 July 1865	A-658
Lafferty, J. H. C.; wife	14 Oct. 1891	G-246
Lafferty. Marshall, head of family	16 May 1867	B-113
Lafranchi, Angelina; Frank	23 Mar. 1921	M-79
Lafranchi, John; Virginia	19 Oct. 1895	H-304
Lairamore, James W.; wife	4 Sep. 1895	H-279
Lake, Helen M.; Wm. D.	1 June 1886	F-268
Laloli, Mrs. Sophie; N.	31 Aug. 1904	J-29
Lamance, Augusta M.; Geo. W.	18 Aug. 1909	K-249
Lamance, J. C., married	5 May 1863	A-552
Lamb, Downing; Elizabeth	1 Oct. 1866	B-33
Lamb, Horace (widow, Perces 4/19/1869, B-319, Chas. C.,	5 Nov. 1862	A-516
Lamb, Rachael, married	21 Mar. 1872	C-63
Lambert, Emma, divorced widow of W. H., minor Orval	6 Dec. 1915	L-238
Lambert, Rebecca, widow of Silvanus D.	18 Mar. 1864	A-595
Lambert, Sarah J.; Richard	1 Mar. 1867	B-88
Lambert, Vincent D.; married	20 Apr. 1861	A-354
Lamkin, Abern A., married	8 Feb. 1875	C-369
Lamonte, Sarah; Herbert	6 July 1910	K-327
Lancaster, William, married	17 June 1876	C-532
Lancaster, Wm; Maria	2 Oct. 1868	B-269
Lancel, Melaine Hubert; Anseline, husband; probate	11 Nov. 1891	E-261
Landes, Goldie; R.	9 Dec. 1891	G-285
Landis, John; Blanche M.	9 May 1911	K-378
Lane, Ann; Walter W.	15 Apr. 1889	F-556
Lane, Delia, married (formerly Delia Cronin)	17 Apr. 1867	B-102
Lane, Mrs. M. A.; M. A.	9 Nov. 1901	I-361
Langdon, C. W.; Eliza Jane	6 Oct. 1862	A-510
Langdon, Nora; C. W.	16 Dec. 1869	B-372
Langsley, Sarah A.; Albert	22 July 1910	K-329
Lanoir, Augustine; Alex	3 Oct. 1912	K-455
Lapum, Harriet A.; Hicks	26 May 1896	H-429
Larison, Eliz.; husband	8 Nov. 1880	E-47
Larison, Saml., married	11 Oct. 1875	C-443
Larkin, Cynthia A.; Seth (12/22/1881, E-174)	7 Feb. 1872	C-41
Larkin, Emma J.; Geo. H.	7 Dec. 1899	I-229

Applicant and Family Information	Filing Date	Vol.-Pg.
Larrabee, Hester A., widow	10 Mar. 1897	H-555
Larsen, Gertrude; Axel O.	14 June 1920	M-40
Larsen, John; wife	21 Sep. 1904	J-32
Larsen, Olef; Caroline Johnson Larsen, wife	15 Jan. 1864	A-582
Lashier, F. A.; Clara E.	28 Dec. 1907	K-87
Lass, Henry F.; wife	21 Feb. 1899	I-186
Latapie, Edward, married	3 Nov. 1873	C-252
Latimer, L. D., married	5 Jan. 1861	A-99
Latimer, Sarah S.; Lorenzo D.	19 Aug. 1893	G-451
Lattanzi, Elena; Emil	19 June 1919	L-482
Laufenberger, Mary; Michael	10 Mar. 1863	A-544
Laughery, Henry, married	4 Aug. 1866	B-31
Laughlin, J. P.; wife	16 Nov. 1904	J-45
Laughlin, J. M.; Sara C.	11 Apr. 1908	K-114
Laughlin, J. W.; Mary L.	22 Apr. 1912	K-422
Laughlin, James H.; Frances E.	24 Apr. 1861	A-267
Laughlin, John M.; Matilda	20 Apr. 1861	A-276
Laughlin, Marshall N., married	24 May 1876	C-522
Laurenzi, Catherine; Placito	24 Aug. 1917	L-365
Lauteren, A. M.; F., husband	5 Oct. 1885	F-144
Laux, Hermann; wife	5 July 1892	G-319
Lavin, Mary; James (4/16/1885, F-45; 8/16/1889, F-594; 8/17/1891, E-200, probate)	25 June 1867	B-122
Lavine, Fannie E.; Frank	12 June 1882	E-230
Lawler, Catharine; James	18 Jan. 1867	B-78
Lawrence, George, married	21 Dec. 1866	B-55
Lawrence, Julia D.	10 Nov. 1914	L-112
Lawrence, L. B.; Nannie L.	29 Aug. 1883	E-372
Lay, Henry D., Jr., married	10 Feb. 1866	A-693
Leal, Antonio A.; wife	3 Jan. 1898	I-39
Leard, Arminta A.; husband	26 Jan. 1879	D-497
Leary, James, head of family; 2 minor children	19 Oct. 1870	B-459
Leary, Thomas; Bridget O.	2 Dec. 1869	B-368
Leary, Wm., married	3 Oct. 1871	C-16
Leavenworth, T. M.; wife Cornelia F. (12/14/1895, F-174; 9/5/1893, probate)	29 Sep. 1883	E-384
LeBaron, Frances Margaret; Harrison M.	29 June 1918	L-412
LeBrun, M. A.; Isabella	20 Mar. 1909	K-214
Leclerc, Lucie B.; Geo. A.	11 June 1894	H-57

Applicant and Family Information	Filing Date	Vol.-Pg.
Leddy, Kate; Patrick	12 Sep. 1899	I-216
Lee, William G., head of family	7 Nov. 1865	A-684
Leek, Jessie V.; Geo. W.	25 Sep. 1893	G-465
Leek, Josephine; Wm. G.	5 Aug. 1885	F-108
Leeta, Margaret; Orton R. (2/21/1899, I-185)	29 Jan. 1896	H-373
Lefebvre, Isabella E.; O. M.	29 Oct. 1894	H-102
Lefurgey, Helen M.; O. B. (11/7/1918, L-446)	28 Nov. 1914	L-118
Legge, Thomas; family	13 Dec. 1878	D-365
Leggerini, Martin; Lauretta V.	23 Feb. 1921	M-75
Leiby, Fannie K.; Geo.	28 Aug. 1883	E-368
Leloh, Salina; F. O.	1 Aug. 1919	L-488
Lemmon, Ida G.; Fred G.	6 Jan. 1919	L-452
Lensey, John, married	6 Sep. 1876	C-552
Leonard, Esther; John	20 Apr. 1878	D-252
Leonard, Michael, single	18 Oct. 1875	C-446
Leonardini, Maria; Paolo; 3 children (9/28/1914, L-107)	4 Dec. 1907	K-84
Leslie, Jonathan, unmarried	4 Dec. 1867	B-173
Leveroni, Caterina, head of household; 5 minors	18 Sep. 1891	G-229
Levy, Susie; Mark	19 July 1913	L-14
Lewis, Anna Amanda, widow; Wm. F. (3/9/1899, I-189)	8 May 1893	G-420
Lewis, C. Lewis, widower	1 Apr. 1861	A-189
Lewis, E. A., married ("Vermont," 2/12/1870, B-379)	23 Jan. 1872	C-32
Lewis, Hiram H.; Mary	2 Apr. 1861	A-200
Lewis, John M.; Jane	8 Apr. 1871	B-510
Lewis, John H., single	25 Apr. 1873	C-147
Lewis, John M., married	29 Apr. 1868	B-230
Lewis, John; Hattie M.	27 June 1878	D-275
Lewis, Martin; Nancy (1/8/1872, C-26)	11 Apr. 1861	A-211
Lewis, Mary M., widow	28 Mar. 1882	E-200
Lewis, R. E.; wife	21 Feb. 1881	E-75
Ley, Henry D., married	5 Oct. 1868	B-268
Lichau, Mary; Albert E.	13 Feb. 1907	K-32
Liddy, Kate	4 Apr. 1890	F-629
Light, Emanual; Elizabeth Emily	2 Nov. 1860	A-59
Lightner, John M.; wife (Sarah, widow, 12/19/1882, E-293)	7 Oct. 1881	E-148
Likens, Amy J.; J. W. (7/30/1877, C-586)	19 Apr. 1876	C-510
Likens, Eliza Ann; Levi (1/30/1886, F-215)	30 Oct. 1880	E-42
Lind, Niles J.; Pearl	26 July 1917	L-360

Applicant and Family Information	Filing Date	Vol.-Pg.
Lindley, Livah S.; Isaac N.	16 Oct. 1895	H-297
Lindley, Nellie; Chas. O.	1 Dec. 1904	J-46
Lindner, Gustave; Marie	20 July 1908	K-145
Lindsay, Mary Ann; J. C. (10/6/1906, K-5)	15 Oct. 1903	I-480
Linebaugh, John; Catherine	19 Nov. 1862	A-520
Linihan, Catharine; J., husband	9 Jan. 1873	B-624
Linshan, Mary; Daniel I.	16 Dec. 1868	B-298
Linsley, Winfield S.; wife	15 June 1889	F-586
Lippert, Edward F.; Emma Gray	30 Nov. 1915	L-235
Lippitt, Edward S., married	23 July 1867	B-132
Lippman, Leo; Mary F. (10/20/1919, M-6)	21 Oct. 1916	L-311
Liss, Magdalena; Carl	19 Aug. 1912	K-443
Litchfield, Eliz. M.; Durant	15 May 1896	H-416
Litchfield, Elmer, no family mentioned (Ester 6/13/1907-K-53)	7 Aug. 1893	G-447
Little, John F.; wife	19 Aug. 1893	G-453
Littlejohn, Anna; Ira J.	5 Jan. 1911	K-358
Litton, E. E., widow (Jackson P. dec'd 24 Oct. 1884; no children); probate	13 July 1885	D-128
Litzins, Louis; wife	14 Feb. 1895	H-171
Lively, John W.; wife; 2 children	6 Mar. 1876	C-502
Livey, Charles R., married	4 Oct. 1866	B-19
Lloyd, John C.; wife	16 Oct. 1895	H-299
Lloyd, William, head of family	5 Feb. 1862	A-399
Lobo, Rosa; J. L.	19 July 1892	G-325
Locatelli, Erminia; Faust	1 Oct. 1908	K-172
Loch, James N.; America	7 Oct. 1867	B-140
Lockie, Mary; John R.	18 Feb. 1918	L-397
Locknane, M. B., married	11 Apr. 1862	A-435
Lockwood, Armeda E.; Nelson	28 Mar. 1887	F-382
Lockwood, John E., married	11 Sep. 1872	C-606
Loftus, Mary; Patrick; probate	23 Apr. 1894	F-103
Loftus, Wm.; Margaret T.	8 Aug. 1903	I-460
Lombard, Fred; Georgia E.	8 Feb. 1910	K-295
Lombardi, Amelia; Severino	9 Aug. 1897	H-604
Lomont, A. A.; Elizabeth	6 Nov. 1880	E-45
Long, Aaron S.; Mariam W.	11 Jan. 1879	D-373
Long, F. M.; family	6 June 1866	B-18
Long, Frederick; married	2 Apr. 1873	C-141

Applicant and Family Information	Filing Date	Vol.-Pg.
Long, Jeremiah; Mary	30 Apr. 1878	D-257
Long, Marguerite A.; M. H.	17 Nov. 1920	M-60
Long, Mary C.; John	4 Nov. 1910	K-344
Longley, Sylvia R.; Frank M.	21 Oct. 1908	K-174
Longly, Mary; R. G.	13 Aug. 1886	F-298
Lonigo, Helen; Emile V.	22 June 1896	H-440
Looney, Robert; Sarah	13 Aug. 1866	B-36
Lopez, Minnie; Antonio B., dec'd; 3 minors; probate	21 Feb. 1898	G-103
Lopus, Frank R.; Mary	23 Dec, 1920	M-66
Lopus, Minnie; John	8 Sep. 1916	L-302
Lorch, John M., married	10 Aug. 1877	C-583
Lorentzen, Lorentz; Emma D.	5 Apr. 1920	M-28
Lott, Fannie J.; James F.	7 Apr. 1900	I-264
Lottritz, Maria Eliz.; widow of John	3 May 1895	H-215
Loud, A. C.; Emily S.	3 Jan. 1871	B-482
Loughery, F. X.; wife	20 June 1885	F-80
Loughnane, James; Mary Ann	26 Dec. 1889	E-613
Lounibos, Bertha Marie; Emile Paul	17 Oct. 1917	L-376
Lovejoy, A. P.; married (11/14/1867, B-153; 8/24/1878, D-312)	16 Oct. 1865	A-679
Lovejoy, George E., married	5 Aug. 1868	B-254
Lovejoy, John, married	28 Sep. 1860	A-43
Lovejoy, Moses; Charlotte	4 Apr. 1868	B-218
Low, Carrie B.; Chas. A.	18 Dec. 1899	I-235
Lowrey, Martha M.; Robert L. (1/22/1914, L-55; 4/14/1915, L-161)	29 Jan. 1913	K-485
Lowry, George W.; married	5 Apr. 1873	C-142
Loyd, Catherine W.; Wm. L.	28 Feb. 1896	H-387
Lubeck, C. W. (K of Powers & C for Deeds)	20 July 1853	K-80
Ludemann, Anna; John	11 Sep. 1894	C-492
Ludolph, Marie; married	18 Oct. 1873	C-249
Ludwig, Thomas J., married	9 May 1877	D-122
Ludy, Carolina; Herman	8 Oct. 1903	I-476
Luff, Eva C., unmarried; head of family; 2 children; Genevieve Dalton, & Hale	18 May 1914	L-79
Lumsden, Helen L.; A. M., dec'd	1 Feb. 1909	K-203
Lusk, Nannie T.; Wm.	29 Apr. 1913	K-499
Lutgens, Henry C.; Lizzie	2 Jan. 1920	M-16
Lutgens, John, married	18 Feb. 1861	A-123
Lutz, Celia; Israel	9 July 1920	M-42

Applicant and Family Information	Filing Date	Vol.-Pg.
Lyman, Oma E.; Jas. H.	3 July 1916	L-289
Lyon, Albert G.; Prudence	9 Sep. 1872	B-604
Lyon, Hattie E.; Chas. E.	3 Apr. 1916	L-268
Lyon, Mary E.; Earl T.	29 June 1917	L-359
Lyon, R. B.; family	24 Mar. 1862	A-412
Lyons, Agnes; Thos. M. (5/10/1900, I-271)	14 Aug. 1893	G-449
Lyttaker, Ballariah J.; R. G.	27 Nov. 1882	F-6
Lyttaker, F. E.; Maria	30 Mar. 1861	A-194
Lyttaker, Marier; Finis Ewing	11 Sep. 1894	G-495
Lyttle, Lottie Lee, head of family (Mother)	10 Dec. 1900	I-307

Applicant and Family Information	Filing Date	Vol.-Pg.
MacDonald, Mattie F.; Alexander S.	10 Mar. 1908	K-110
MacGregor, Matha J.; A. P.	20 Oct. 1896	H-499
MacKenzie, Annie S.; Alexander G.	10 Mar. 1908	K-109
MacKenzie, Margaret A. (formerly Carter); Richard F.	30 Dec. 1914	L-127
Mackey, Addie May, married	10 Nov. 1873	C-256
Mackey, Emily; Geo. Herbert	4 Dec. 1915	L-244
MacKillop, Donald V.; Emma	4 Dec. 1916	L-319
Macy, Hiram; family	9 Oct. 1879	D-468
Macy, Wm. M.; Vesta S.	11 Apr. 1861	A-218
Maddalena, A.; wife	28 Mar. 1889	F-547
Maddux, W. H.; wife	4 Jan. 1883	E-297
Madison, J. H.; Charlotte R.	2 Oct. 1911	K-393
Madsen, Emilie K.; H. H. (11/16/1899, I-223)	1 Nov. 1894	H-110
Maede, August, married	17 Jan. 1878	D-200
Maffei, Angelina; Italo	4 June 1906	J-131
Magee, Thos. W.; wife	18 Dec. 1895	H-334
Magg, Frank; wife	3 May 1886	F-251
Mahan, Jno.; Rebecky	10 Apr. 1861	A-207
Mahoney, John; Mary Ann	21 Oct. 1870	B-460
Mails, Claudia M.; Wm.	2 Apr. 1892	G-306
Main, Mary E.; James A.	21 Dec. 1916	L-321
Mallory, Andrew P.; Harriet C.	13 Aug. 1864	A-616
Mallory, George B.; Juniatta	14 Dec. 1909	K-281
Malnick, Samuel	14 Aug. 1906	J-147
Maloney, David; Ellen	23 Oct. 1868	B-273
Maloney, Patrick; Mary	6 Jan. 1874	C-238
Manchester, Emeline C.; Edmund F.	17 June 1905	J-77
Mane, Anna; James	16 June 1916	L-285
Mangin, Gladyst M.; Eugene L.	15 Mar. 1907	K-35
Mann, Edwin E.; Elzina E.	22 Mar. 1920	M-23
Mann, H. L.; Ida M.	3 Sep. 1908	K-162
Mann, Lafayett L.; Martha Ann	11 Nov. 1861	A-384
Mann, Mary; John (4/17/1863, A-548; 4/14/1868, B-223)	24 Mar. 1862	A-414
Mann, Wm. D., married; family	15 Apr. 1875	C-383
Manning, John, married	2 Dec. 1868	B-283
Mansfield, Mrs. F. M., widow; 2 minors	2 June 1876	C-528
Mansfield, Lyons (Note: Book B lost); probate	12 Aug. 1869	B-43
Mansfield, Sophia, widow	12 July 1869	B-341

Applicant and Family Information	Filing Date	Vol.-Pg.
Mardon, Henry R.; Emma	25 Apr. 1861	A-304
Marks, Benj., married	11 May 1869	B-331
Marris, Ernest A.; Minnie E.	30 Nov. 1914	L-119
Manuel, H. C.; Nettie	15 May 1894	H-50
Marall (Maral), Mary; Frank S.	1 June 1901	I-332
March, Sarah E.; Wm. J.	14 Apr. 1868	B-222
Marcill, Napoleon; wife	20 Nov. 1891	G-271
Marris, Ernest A.	8 Dec. 1913	L-45
Marshall, Mrs. F. L.; Frank L.	8 Jan. 1897	H-520
Marshall, Hattie L.; Thos. H.	9 June 1917	L-352
Marshall, John; wife	10 Feb. 1880	D-520
Marshall, Nannie; Wm. H.	31 May 1906	J-132
Marks, Berry, married	4 June 1870	B-412
Maroni, P.; wife	12 Sep. 1895	H-284
Maroni, Peter; wife	24 Feb. 1908	K-100
Marsh, Rachel B.; Henry	10 Aug. 1881	E-129
Marshall, E. B.; married	1 Oct. 1873	C-228
Marshall, Henry; Sarah	12 June 1883	E-343
Marshall, Sarah A.; married (est. of John, 1/2/1883, E-298)	27 May 1873	C-164
Marthisen, W. D.; Ethel	27 Apr. 1916	L-273
Marti, Eliz. J.; Melchior, dec'd, probate	1 June 1898	G-168
Martin, Angeline B.; J. M.	13 Nov. 1878	D-353
Martin, Christian Julius; Lurena Florence	9 Mar. 1916	L-260
Martin, Hattie B.; Eugene E.	1 Sep. 1888	F-501
Martin, James; Mary Ann	17 Apr. 1861	A-238
Martin, John S.; wife	14 Oct. 1882	E-275
Martin, John S., Jr.; family	24 Feb. 1880	E-10
Martin, Lillie E.; Wm. K.	23 Nov. 1905	J-110
Martin, Mary Ann; S. B.	3 Jan. 1868	B-179
Martino, Giovannoni; wife	5 Dec. 1887	F-433
Mascherini, Maria; Faust E.	23 Feb. 1910	K-298
Mason, Centhia; Frank L.	27 Sep. 1900	I-294
Mason, Julia M.; William	3 Oct. 1912	K-456
Mason, Serena H., married	13 Mar. 1875	D-18
Mast, Sarah E.; family	7 Apr. 1880	D-549
Mathe, Georgina, widow of Louis	13 Jan. 1900	I-239
Mather, Kittie; Wm.	6 Jan. 1888	F-442
Mather, William; wife	24 May 1907	K-43

Applicant and Family Information	Filing Date	Vol.-Pg.
Mathers, L. H.; Katie S.	14 Mar. 1916	L-262
Mathews, Alfred F.; Mary Frances	24 Dec. 1868	B-301
Mathews, John, married	8 Apr. 1873	C-144
Mathews, M. H., widow	21 May 1881	E-101
Mathewson, Harley P.; wife	5 Sep. 1905	J-96
Mathewson, Maria A.; Roderick (1/9/1861, abandonment, A-102)	24 Feb. 1862	A-405
Mathisen, Charles S.; wife	18 Jan. 1881	E-65
Matson, Mary M.; Jacob	1 Oct. 1885	F-140
Matthews, Alfred F., Mary F. (9/2/1871, B-556)	5 Feb. 1868	B-196
Matthews, Elias M.; Juliet	25 Apr. 1861	A-337
Matthews, Mary Ellen; John J.	14 Oct. 1895	H-294
Matthews, Eliza; Geo. J.	12 Jan. 1888	F-445
Matthies, Lina; Heinrich	10 Aug. 1880	E-28
Matthews, O. B.; Taliatha (7/3/1866, A-706)	26 Apr. 1862	A-470
Matteson, Alvin C.; Lottie D.	10 Nov. 1911	K-400
Matteucci, Lawrence; Emma C.	4 Dec. 1916	L-317
Matthies, Lina; Heinrich	13 Nov. 1882	E-282
Mauch, Mrs. Dora; Adam	19 July 1902	I-407
Maxwell, C. L.; wife (6/9/1884, F-7)	28 May 1884	E-476
Maxwell, J. G.; Annie M.	18 Apr. 1861	A-243
Maxwell, John M.; Clara L.	18 Feb. 1861	A-129
May, J. J.; Mary L.	7 Apr. 1862	A-425
May, Mary C.; Hugh S.	5 Sep. 1862	A-502
Mayer, Lewis W.; family	18 Sep. 1871	B-560
Mayfield, Geo. W.; wife	5 Jan. 1885	E-542
Mayfield, Lucy A.; Geo. W.	12 Sep. 1914	L-101
Maynard, May; Harry H.	22 Apr. 1895	H-213
Mazota, Ellen/Hellen; Louis; child Lilly May (8/20/1878, D-310)	8 June 1874	C-310
Mazza, Ralph; Olive	27 Nov. 1916	L-316
McAndrus, P., widower; 5 children	28 July 1888	F-482
McAskill, Maggie; Angus	8 Apr. 1897	H-566
McAuliffe, Helen; P.	11 Oct. 1899	I-220
McBean, Mary Anne, widow	8 Dec. 1881	E-169
McBride, Murrie J.; Mary E.	2 Sep. 1896	H-480
McCain, Geo. W.; Margaret Ann (C-275)	11 Jan. 1868	B-307
McCallum, Geo. S. Kellie; wife	13 Jan. 1896	H-358
McCallum, H.; wife	20 Apr. 1861	A-288

Applicant and Family Information	Filing Date	Vol.-Pg.
McCann, Ellen; John (6/13/1891, E-170, probate)	16 July 1879	D-434
McCappin, Lavina; James	17 Oct. 1898	I-135
McCargar, Hugh S.; Minnie E.; 2 minors (K-120)	12 Mar. 1908	K-111
McCarcy, Myrtle A.; Harry	17 Dec. 1920	M-64
McCarthy, Mary E.	18 May 1901	I-330
McCarthy, Michael; Bridged	20 July 1866	B-1
McCartney, Sarah L.; James	15 Feb. 1908	K-97
McCarty, Catherine, widow of Andrew	29 Oct. 1892	G-364
McCarty, Mary; Wm.	15 Oct. 1884	E-514
McCarty, Mortimer, married	29 Mar. 1870	B-392
McCaughy, Nancy; James	1 Mar. 1898	I-58
McChristian, Sarah; Patrick	15 July 1878	D-294
McChristian, Viola F.; Wm. E.	6 Sep. 1898	I-116
McClish, Thomas	Apr. 186_	
McClure, Mrs. F. L.; Nathaniel C.	7 Apr. 1909	K-222
McConathy, James; Mrs. F. A.	27 June 1882	E-23
McCoy, Elizabeth; John	18 Sep. 1871	B-561
McCracken, J. C.; Rebecca	14 July 1868	B-250
McCrae, Emma C.; Josephine; James, dec'd	27 Sep. 1893	F-1
McCray, Frances C.; Warren; probate	27 Mar. 1899	I-196
McCready, Samuel, married	3 Sep. 1877	D-143
McCulloch, Harriet E.; Robert (2/7/1885, F-21)	19 July 1880	D-588
McCullum, John A.; Mary P.	7 Aug. 1880	K-66
McCutchan, Angeline; David M.; 3 minors	18 June 1883	C-532
McCutchan, Stanley; Elizabeth M. (6/3/1915, L-181); probate	6 June 1913	L-6
McCutchan, Mary P.; George F.	10 Oct. 1916	L-307
McDaniel, Wm.; Elizabeth H. (L-66)	6 Jan. 1913	K-480
McDermott, Wm.; Betsey	17 June 1882	E-245
McDonald, John; Catherine	28 Dec. 1880	E-58
McDonald, Donald; Louisa D. (A-190)	28 Sep. 1860	A-30
McDonald, Frank; wife	16 Oct. 1893	H-4
McDonald, John; Catherine	2 Sep. 1878	D-315
McDonald, Thomas; Ora Brittain (minor child)	2 July 1913	L-11
McDonald, Peter; Sarah	18 June 1870	B-418
McDonell, Maggie; R. A.	26 Feb. 1881	E-80
McDougal, Susannah; Peter	18 May 1885	F-54
McElhany, Maggie; Speer	24 Aug. 1892	G-339
McFadgen, Allen, married	9 Nov. 1877	D-174

Applicant and Family Information	Filing Date	Vol.-Pg.
McFarland, Alexander, married	19 Dec. 1868	B-300
McFee, Anna Margaritte, widow	4 Dec. 1912	K-474
McGaha, Andrew J.; Mary E. (2 children)	8 June 1915	L-182
McGee, Robert; Hanorah	5 May 1870	B-405
McGee, H. W., married	21 June 1873	C-177
McGee, Henry W.; Sarah A.	16 Sep. 1864	A-618
McGee, James H., married	19 Sep. 1873	C-224
McGee, Robert (no family)	5 Nov. 1878	D-350
McGinty, James	5 Mar. 1887	F-363
McGeorge, Robert; wife	19 Mar. 1884	E-451
McGeorge, Robt., unmarried	19 Jan. 1892	G-296
McGhan, Martin, married	23 Sep. 1871	B-565
McGovern, Freda; John Joseph	21 Jan. 1918	L-394
McGovern, Mrs. Katie L.; Daniel	4 Apr. 1894	H-45
McGraul, Michael, married	8 June 1868	B-240
McGregor, Wm. K.; Mrs. Anna	29 May 1886	F-265
McGrew, J. C.; Sophia	7 Oct. 1884	E-512
McGuire, Cloie A.; Thomas	11 May 1893	G-422
McGuire, Cornelius, married	1 Feb. 1876	C-486
McGuire, Margaret; John	2 Apr. 1878	D-244
McHarvey, Chas.; Avilla A.	25 Apr. 1861	A-329
McHenry, James; Sarah D. Pearce, wife	15 Nov. 1860	A-57
McIlmoil, Almira L.; John	14 Mar. 1878	D-236
McIntosh, J. E.; Margaret	19 July 1865	A-662
McIntosh, John Edward; wife	19 Feb. 1861	A-136
McIsaac, Margaret; Alexander	1 Oct. 1892	G-356
McKay, Angus, married (5/17/1867,B-117)	24 Nov. 1865	A-686
McKeadney, Katie; Hugh (dec'd), (2/9/1903, H-138, probate)	26 May 1883	E-340
McKee, Samuel H.; Mary Isabelle	5 June 1913	L-5
McKenzie, James; wife	8 Dec. 1881	E-167
McKenzie, John Washington; wife	19 Sep. 1891	G-234
McKenzie, Wm. A., unmarried	25 Feb. 1879	D-385
McKenzie, Winefred A.	13 Apr. 1875	C-381
McKillap, Dugald; Huldah G.	9 Jan. 1914	L-54
McLane, Addie; Charles A.	7 Oct. 1915	L-219
McLean, Annie/Anna; Donald (1/2/1891, G-152)	10 Aug. 1886	F-296
McLean, Mrs. Ellen M.; widow	1 Apr. 1880	D-546
McLean, H. M.; wife	13 July 1885	F-95

Applicant and Family Information	Filing Date	Vol.-Pg.
McLennan, Dora; M. K.	10 Nov. 1887	F-428
McLeod, Daniel; Elizabeth W.	23 Apr. 1861	A-273
McLeod, Mary Helen; John A.	20 May 1914	L-177
McMannis, Retena H.; Thomas J.	15 Feb. 1918	L-396
McMannus, Eliza Jane; J. G.	22 Mar. 1877	D-99
McMillen, Margaret, widow	1 Nov. 1880	E-44
McMinn, John; wife	14 Apr. 1880	D-560
McMullen, Bridget; John (6/4/1890, D-556, probate)	30 Apr. 1888	F-466
McMullen, Daniel; married	19 Oct. 1877	D-168
McMurray, Amanda; E. L.	3 Aug. 1863	A-560
McMurray, Elijah S., head of family	17 Oct. 1866	B-25-26
McNabb, James H., head of family of 4 children	8 June 1895	H-227
McNally, Mary; Michael (2/18/1884, Mary dec'd. E-442 decree)	24 May 1871	B-526
McNamara, Barney; Harrich/Harriet O'Rourke, wf. (4/15/1871, B-511)	18 Dec. 1869	B-73
McNeil, Zephra A.; Silas W.	26 Aug. 1898	I-110
McNeill, John , married	6 Nov. 1871	B-574
McPherson, Early; wife	18 Dec. 1893	C-484
McPherson, Lycursus; wife (insolvent debtor, 10/17/1881, F-4)	19 Aug. 1880	D-557
McPherson, Perry L.; Margaret J.	8 Aug. 1914	L-94
McReynolds, James; Anna	16 Oct. 1876	D-45
McReynolds, Emma; Sam'l	22 Jan. 1896	H-363
McReynolds, Wm.; family	21 Oct. 1879	D-477
McRossie, Jane; James	20 Sep. 1881	E-136
Meacham, Eliz. A.; Geo.	29 Apr. 1897	H-581
Meacham, Sarah J.; Alonzo (8/25/1875, C-433)	11 Sep. 1854	R-1
Mead, James A., married	24 July 1879	D-438
Mead, W. H., married; family	27 Apr. 1875	C-387
Mead, W. R., married; family	2 June 1875	C-407
Mead, Wm; Catherine	6 May 1861	A-364
Meadors, Peter H.; wife	9 Sep. 1879	D-460
Meadows, Mollie A.; widow of Peter H.	20 Mar. 1901	I-319
Means, J. S.; Kate	29 Jan. 1890	G-3
Meddock, Jesse T.; wife Hermuna	30 Jan. 1905	J-54
Medley, A. G., married	26 Oct. 1867	B-155
Meehan, Catherine; Patrick	14 Jan. 1887	E-572
Meehan, Patrick, married	17 Aug. 1865	D-212
Meek, Alice; W. E. (11/6/1911, K-399; 11/11/1914, L-114)	25 Aug. 1909	K-251

Applicant and Family Information	Filing Date	Vol.-Pg.
Meeker, J. O., head of family, unmarried	19 Sep. 1903	I-470
Meeker, Melvin C.; wife Flavia	22 July 1873	C-196
Mego, Tony; wife	30 Mar. 1898	I-63
Meier, Minna; Gustav	11 Sep. 1915	L-213
Melehan, Ellen Gertrude, head of fam.; incl. father, unmarried sister	13 Aug. 1908	K-155
Mellehan, Mariah; P.	18 July 1876	C-541
Mello, Frank J.; Leeta	27 Jan. 1914	L-57
Melson, Emma; John	7 May 1878	D-259
Mendenhall, J. G.; Margaret	3 Feb. 1911	K-365
Menefie, Drucella, widow	9 Apr. 1862	A-428
Meneray, Emma P.; P. A.	4 Dec. 1915	L-237
Menne, Frank; wife	10 Jan. 1911	K-359
Mentzer, P. B., dec'd; Annie E., probate	10 Apr. 1889	D-481
Merchant, Joel; wf.Mary Ellen	7 Mar. 1865	A-642
Merchant, Mary Louisa; Thos. Sam'l	7 Feb. 1895	H-167
Meridith, Margaret E.; Cyrus U. (3/20/1895; H-194; 8/14/1897, H-608; 8/21/1897, H-613)	17 Sep. 1890	G-116
Merker, John; Anne	19 July 1876	C-543
Merritt, Louise B., div. from F. A.; children: Marguerite, 14; Mary Burd, 11	27 Jan. 1908	K-95
Merritt, Mary; John	30 Aug. 1897	H-623
Messerli, Gotlieb; Elizabeth	13 June 1890	G-51
Metcalf, S. W., married	18 Nov. 1876	D-56
Metzenbach, Wm. B.; Emma W.	10 Oct. 1879	D-471
Metzger, Augusta; Wm.	22 Aug. 1887	F-410
Metzger, Mrs. Wilnar E.; Joseph E. (7/7/1888, F-476; 9/13/1888, F-505; Joseph insolvent 12/3/1889, E-606)	2 Jan. 1886	F-191
Metzler, Dorothea, married	27 Sep. 1872	D-6
Metzler, Theo. C., married	4 May 1872	C-92
Meyer, Bertha G.; Lawrence	26 Jan. 1901	I-314
Meyer, Claus; wife	17 May 1884	E-470
Meyer, Samuel; Dora (8/29/1885, F-117; 11/12/1886, F-326)	3 Nov. 1882	E-278
Meyer, Carl; Mrs. Elizabeth	10 June 1905	J-76
Meyer, Jacob F.; Barbetta, dec'd (8/2/1897, F-619, probate)	23 Jan. 1884	E-424
Meyer, Johanna; Anton, probate	8 June 1896	F-433
Meyer, Lorentz, married	29 Mar. 1875	C-379
Meyer, Samuel, married	11 Aug. 1870	B-442
Michael, Emma A., married	15 May 1874	B-644

Applicant and Family Information	Filing Date	Vol.-Pg.
Micheli, Charles; Mrs. Marguerite (4/30/1887, F-389)	26 July 1886	F-294
Middleton, Emilie; W. H.	21 Dec. 1860	A-88
Middleton, J. H.; wife	5 June 1899	I-208
Middleton, Walter V.; wife	13 Jan. 1880	D-505
Middleton, William T.; Nancy J.	2 Jan. 1861	A-79
Middleton, Zacharias; Z. A.	4 Aug. 1870	B-436
Migo, Rosa; Manuel	8 Oct. 1889	E-593
Miller, Margaret; James	12 June 1885	F-74
Miller, Adam; wife (1/9/1891, G-159)	9 Apr. 1890	G-35
Miller, Anthony, married	12 Oct. 1869	B-353
Miller, Bertha; John	15 Nov. 1877	D-175
Miller, B. P.; Cora L.	19 Jan. 1894	H-21
Miller, Elizabeth E. LeGrand, widow	16 July 1907	K-58
Miller, Francis M., married	10 Sep. 1872	C-120
Miller, George; Celia	4 May 1864	A-607
Miller, Chas.; Hattie M.	13 Dec. 1899	I-231
Miller, Hiram B.; Jennie E.	3 Apr. 1900	I-263
Miller, James; Martha Jane	5 May 1863	A-551
Miller, Jennie; Chas. R.	1 July 1902	I-400
Miller, J. D.; Eliz. LeGrand, wife	10 Apr. 1869	B-323
Miller, Joel; Charlotte	7 Dec. 1860	A-72
Miller, John F.; Exor, wife	10 Feb. 1916	L-234
Miller, Jno. Talitha C.	23 Apr. 1861	A-327
Miller, John D.; wife (10/27/1891, G-253)	23 July 1885	F-101
Miller, John D.; Elizabeth E.; minors (10/3/1873, C-229)	20 June 1873	C-173
Miller, J. W.; wife	21 Feb. 1898	I-56
Miller, Lydia F., widow	2 Nov. 1887	F-426
Miller, Martha M.; J. M.	8 Jan. 1896	H-345
Miller, Mary E.; Geo. E.	6 Dec. 1883	E-405
Miller, Mrs. Nellie C.; Geo. M.	22 Sep. 1909	K-263
Miller, R. W.; wife	24 Aug. 1900	I-285
Miller, Saul; Sarah Margaret	29 Feb. 1872	C-55
Miller, Teresa; Jacob	2 Dec. 1910	K-350
Miller, Tom; Maud	1 Nov. 1920	M-55
Miller, Wayne D. L.; wife (1/30/1895, H-145)	30 July 1890	G-79
Millerick, George; Catherine	11 July 1908	K-144
Millerick, Ida L.; Michael	14 Nov. 1910	K-347
Milligan, Dolphus; Elva	1 Nov. 1919	M-9

Applicant and Family Information	Filing Date	Vol.-Pg.
Millikan, Henry L.; Sarah R.	30 June 1882	E-223
Millington, N. Maria, widow of Seth; Ada; Grace; Olivia; Buchanan; Seth, 9 yrs.; John; Zachariah	11 Feb. 1868	B-200
Mills, Andrew; Caroline D.	26 Sep. 1870	B-451
Mills, Andrew (also see bankruptcy action)	7 Sep. 1871	B-537
Mills, A. J.; Nancy	16 Mar. 1861	A-164
Mills, Aurelia C.; John, dec'd	30 Sep. 1909	K-267
Mills, E. H.; wife	25 Jan. 1896	H-365
Mills, L. L.; Grace B.	10 June 1919	L-480
Mills, Mrs. Pauline; Robert	26 Nov. 1915	L-234
Mills, Sarah; Geo.	1 Feb. 1877	D-81
Minor, B. M., married	28 Dec. 1877	D-190
Minto, Carrie E.; T. D.	17 Dec. 1910	K-353
Mintzer, P. B.; wife	29 Oct. 1885	F-153
Miranda, Josefa; Francisco	14 Feb. 1870	B-494
Mishima, Montaro; wife Teru	28 Feb. 1913	K-489
Misner, David R.; wife	29 Apr. 1887	E-579
Missbach, Maria B.; Ernest Albin	2 July 1912	K-439
Mitchell, Hannah; Chas. E.	24 Apr. 1893	G-412
Mitchell, Hurley; E. R., husband	6 July 1915	L-191
Mitchel, Jas. H.; family	20 Sep. 1878	D-328
Mitchell, John H.; family (Sadie a witness)	11 Aug. 1879	D-449
Mitchell, Lucy H.; head of family; 4 minors	30 May 1870	B-409
Mitchell, Margaret A., formerly M. Dunbar, widow of Wm. F.	20 Apr. 1883	E-324
Mitchell, Margaret A.; L. W. (6/11/1884, F-8)	28 Dec. 1883	E-413
Mitoma, Y.; Towa, wife	28 Feb. 1913	K-490
Mize, Merrill, married	17 May 1866	B-6
Moak, Boltis; wf. Boltis, Mary	1 Oct. 1860	A-29
Mobley, Pearl J.; J. Elmer	15 June 1906	J-136
Mock, John L., married	21 July 1873	C-191
Mock, Wesley; wife	10 Oct. 1881	E-149
Moebes, Augusta; August (1/28/1919, L-459)	30 Sep. 1909	K-266
Mohr, Elizabeth; Jacob	9 Jan. 1878	D-196
Moll, Lena; Emile (12/15/1914, L-124)	19 May 1911	K-379
Moller, Henry, married	24 July 1872	C-116
Molleson, Henry P.; wife Mary Fine	6 July 1868	B-244
Moltzen, Detlef Frederick, married; 4 children only mentioned	24 June 1884	F-13
Moniz, Manuel J.; Josephine M.	29 Oct. 1917	L-377

Applicant and Family Information	Filing Date	Vol.-Pg.
Monroe, William; Nancy (abandonment)	11 Sep. 1860	A-24
Monroe, Wm.; wife	24 Apr. 1862	A-455
Montague, Hugh; married; family	31 Dec. 1875	C-473
Moody, Bertha; Clyde L.	8 Oct. 1917	L-373
Moore, Archie S.	15 Dec. 1903	I-486
Moore, R. D.; Catherine E.; no children, probate	21 June 1892	E-350
Moore, Cephas P.; wife	6 Dec. 1893	G-480
Moore, Chas. B.; Cornelia	18 Nov. 1871	C-3
Moore, Edwin, married	14 Oct. 1873	C-244
Moore, Electa; C. P., husband	7 July 1877	C-567
Moore, Elvina; Austin (10/14/1912, K-460)	27 July 1908	K-149
Moore, Eudora E.; Thos. B.	7 Mar. 1900	I-255
Moore, Mattie N.	27 Sep. 1920	M-51
Moore, Mrs. Naomi; Cephas P.	5 Dec. 1896	H-511
Moore, R. D.; Catherine E.	6 Mar. 1872	D-1
Moran, Eliz. J., widow	13 Aug. 1884	E-497
Morce, James Edwin; family	15 May 1880	D-572
Moreland, Alice B.; W. W.	2 Mar. 1891	G-170
Moretti, Celestina; Achille	2 Dec. 1910	K-351
Moretti, Giovannina; Giuseppe	11 Aug. 1915	L-202
Morey, N. L.; Hannah P.	21 Feb. 1861	A-138
Morgan, Bridget, unmarried; family	22 May 1868	B-237
Morgan, Caroline L., Mrs., unmarried, hd. Of family; 2 children & mother	23 May 1914	L-80
Morgan, Geo. A., married	22 Dec. 1877	D-188
Morhbach, Nicholas, dec'd.; Catherine; no children (D-32, 33 & 34, all, probate)	19 Feb. 1883	D-32
Morley, Martha, married	23 Jan. 1878	D-207
Morrill, B. D.; wife; 5 children	29 Sep. 1874	C-333
Morris, Carrie S.; Edward	25 July 1912	K-440
Morris, Joseph H. P.; wife Maria L. (B-76)	23 Apr. 1861	A-258
Morris, Lanna; John	7 Apr. 1862	A-427
Morris, Miles; wife	12 Dec. 1885	F-172
Morris, Sarah E.; J. C.	12 June 1877	C-557
Morris, Wm. H.; Rhoda E.	5 May 1879	D-407
Morissey, Annie R.; John	15 Sep. 1910	K-335
Morrison, G. T.; Estella M.	22 Apr. 1905	J-65
Morrison, Geo. T.; wife	1 Apr. 1903	I-442
Morrison, Hal; Edith	31 July 1915	L-200

Applicant and Family Information	Filing Date	Vol.-Pg.
Morrison, Mahala; S.	12 Sep. 1868	B-263
Morrow, E. E., married	15 May 1877	D-127
Morrow, J. H.; wife	31 Aug. 1885	F-118
Morrow, James, Jr., married	15 May 1877	D-126
Morrow, James, Sr., married	27 Jan. 1877	D-78
Morrow, J., Sr.; Caroline E.	8 July 1881	E-109
Morse, C. W.; Lillie	20 Oct. 1908	K-173
Morse, Daniel P., married	26 Dec. 1871	B-568
Morse, Edgar L.; Bertha E.	25 Feb. 1914	L-63
Morse, Joseph M., married	30 Jan. 1868	B-194
Morshead, Philip; Julia A.	26 July 1901	I-346
Morton, David; Margaret M.	8 Oct. 1867	B-138
Morton, Martin F.; wife	9 Mar. 1894	H-32
Mothorn, D. H.; wife	1 May 1896	H-406
Motkin, Ben	28 June 1917	L-358
Mount, Charles V.; Irene B.	29 May 1914	L-81
Mowbray, Mary J.; married; family	23 Sep. 1875	C-438
Moxon, Margret; Wm. H.	29 Sep. 1892	G-353
Mueller, Minnie; Chas. E.	25 May 1916	L-280
Muff, Eliz.; John	12 Jan. 1895	H-134
Muldry, Martin; wife	20 May 1891	G-193
Mulgrew, Felix; Susana	11 Apr. 1861	A-216
Mulgrew, Mary F.; John F.	26 Feb. 1890	G-15
Mulkey, Sarah N.; David Edward	2 Dec. 1914	L-120
Mull, Eliza I.; Nathan	24 Aug. 1866	B-38
Mullagan, John, married	3 Jan. 1878	D-192
Mullen, Ann; Eli	6 Sep. 1862	A-500
Muller, Carl, married	13 Oct. 1869	B-354
Muller, Mary, widow; John Kasper, dec'd 7/11/1891, intestate	30 July 1906	J-144
Mulligan, John; Maria M.	9 Dec. 1864	A-628
Mullinax, I. G., married	9 May 1871	B-516
Munday, B. B., married	13 July 1870	B-428
Munsell, Sarah H., married	24 Dec. 1864	A-631
Murphy, Catharine, married	7 Nov. 1873	C-255
Murphy, Delia I.; Rufus	9 Oct. 1877	D-160
Murphy, Edward, married	27 Aug. 1866	B-43
Murphy, Mrs. Estelle; Peter Leo; child James Peter	7 May 1915	L-169
Murphy, J. D.; wife	12 May 1880	D-569

Applicant and Family Information	Filing Date	Vol.-Pg.
Murphy, Jeremiah, married	24 Sep. 1867	B-147
Murphy, Nancy J.; Richard W.	30 Sep. 1886	E-564
Murphy, Patrick; Mary	1 Sep. 1868	B-259
Murphy, Wyman; wife	10 Dec. 1878	D-362
Murray, Johanna; Patrick	28 Aug. 1877	C-589
Murray, Joseph; Sallie	16 June 1909	K-235
Murray, Lena L.; Wm. H.	1 Oct. 1898	I-125
Murray, Margaret; Dennis	25 June 1872	C-108
Murray, Patrick, married	10 June 1870	B-416
Murray, Sarah, widow	7 Mar. 1861	A-147
Muther, Fanny M.; Frank (5/6/1886, F-255)	12 Apr. 1880	D-550
Myers, C. S. L.; wife H. M.	29 Jan. 1861	A-113
Myers, C. W.; wife	27 Feb. 1894	H-28
Myers, Jackson R.; Jane E.	22 Apr. 1861	A-260
Myers, Sarah H.; D. P.	18 Dec. 1884	E-529

Applicant and Family Information	Filing Date	Vol.-Pg.
Nagle, Frederick G.; wife (H-262)	12 Nov. 1878	D-352
Nalley, Mrs. Martha E.; A. B.	13 June 1881	E-103
Nardi, Rammira; husband G.	10 Nov. 1913	L-41
Nasse, John; Minnie; 1 child	30 Sep. 1913	L-32
Nathanson, J. C.; wife	20 Oct. 1896	H-497
Nathanson, Martin; Dorathea	28 Mar. 1861	A-195
Nauert, Herman F.; Louise; child	15 Dec. 1913	L-46
Naughton, Hubert; Mary (6/4/1890, D-559, probate)	15 May 1879	D-412
Nay, M. Eltha; Heber L.	20 May 1913	K-505
Nay, L. G.; wife	25 Apr. 1894	G-488
Naylor, Jeanette Bernice; Charles E.	4 Aug. 1915	L-201
Near, Lillian; J. C.	29 Apr. 1902	I-387
Neblette, Edw., married (E-481)	7 July 1868	B-247
Neece, Caroline; A.	30 Nov. 1877	D-177
Needham, Festus, married	24 May 1873	C-149
Neeham, Festus; Mary dec'd	17 July 1907	K-59
Neely, Katie; Thos. L.	5 Dec. 1894	H-117
Nelis, Owen; Catherine (D-9)	24 Feb. 1869	B-315
Nelligan, Marie L.; Joseph R.	8 May 1917	L-346
Nelson, Annie M., widow of James I.; 4 minors	26 Aug. 1914	L-98
Nelson, Darius J., married	3 Apr. 1877	D-101
Nelson, James; wife	22 July 1880	D-596
Nelson, James Iry; Annie May	6 Sep. 1910	K-333
Nelson, Wm. C.; wife	5 Mar. 1881	E-82
Newberry, Cyrus R.; married (3/20/1891, G-177)	3 July 1873	C-185
Newburg, E.; married, family	1 July 1878	D-285
Newburg, Fanny; Edward; probate	13 Nov. 1893	F-18
Newby, Harrison C.; wife	25 Feb. 1885	F-26
Newcom, Gesina; husband Wm. dec'd; children: Edgar, Gertrude, minors	14 Sep. 1909	K-260
Newcomb, Mary A.; C. L.; 2 minors	25 Jan. 1909	K-199
Newell, J. L.; Joseph L.; Gyda V.	23 Dec. 1919	M-15
Newman, Bleistein, married	18 Mar. 1862	A-422
Newton, Mary B.; John A.	7 Feb. 1871	B-493
Neyce, James H.; Ella B. (2/23/1888, F-456)	14 Feb. 1878	D-221
Nichols, Auta Pearl; W. E.	19 Mar. 1910	K-305
Nichols, Mary, widow of Thos A., married 3/19/1872; est. doc. 4048	26 Mar. 1906	J-126
Nickerson, S. C.; Bertha H.	1 Aug. 1905	J-88

Applicant and Family Information	Filing Date	Vol.-Pg.
Nicolai, Herman; Rose; no children	11 Sep. 1909	K-259
Nicoll, Daniel C., married (12/15/1877, D-185)	8 Sep. 1873	C-219
Nielsen, Carl; Hilda B.	8 Sep. 1920	M-48
Nielson, Mary; Niels	27 Apr. 1901	I-324
Nielson, N. P., widower; 2 minors	14 Sep. 1920	M-49
Niestrath, Rose A.; Charles H.	19 Feb. 1908	K-99
Nixon, John L., married	12 Apr. 1873	B-638
Nobec, Adam, married	1 Dec. 1874	C-348
Noble, John F.; wife	14 July 1898	I-99
Nolan, Chas. P.; wife S. J.	19 Mar. 1896	H-392
Nolan, Patrick, married	29 Apr. 1870	B-398
Nonella, Mrs. M. G.; Sylvester	16 Sep. 1914	L-102
Noonan, P. H.; wife	26 Aug. 1891	G-222
Nordbom, Peter G.; Sarah T.	5 July 1867	B-127
Norman, Emelie Rueff, widow of Wm. John; minor dau. Dorothy	19 Aug. 1915	L-206
Norrbom, Sarah T.; Peter G. (B-127; K-420)	1 Oct. 1891	G-240
Norris, Charles, married	23 Apr. 1862	A-454
Norris, Hannah A.; widow of S. A. (now Coon)	24 July 1895	H-245
Norton, Wm; Philinda	23 Mar. 1893	G-400
Norton, William M., married	1 Oct. 1873	C-227
Nosler, H. E.; wife	10 Apr. 1899	I-197
Nottingham, Thomas, married	29 Jan. 1874	C-282
Nottingham, Anna; Wm. T.	9 Nov. 1889	F-622
Nourse, Laura A.; Geo. F.	23 Aug. 1884	E-502
Nowell, Charles W., married	3 Sep. 1877	D-142
Nowell, Mertie M., widow; May Lorraine, 9 yrs; Herbert Warren, 5 yrs.	20 Nov. 1911	K-402
Nowlin, Samuel S., married	29 Oct. 1874	C-338
Nunez, Antonio de Souza; wife	24 Nov. 1879	E-4
Nunes, Clara Florinna; husb. Manuel Jose; minor children: Manuel, Joseph, Frank, Adelia; probate	11 June 1894	F-142
Nunn, Hugh; Sarah M. Rowe Nunn	25 Apr. 1862	A-466

Applicant and Family Information	Filing Date	Vol.-Pg.
Oates, Mattie F.; James W.	22 Aug. 1887	F-408
O'Brien, Catherine; Mathew	16 July 1901	I-343
O'Brien, Isabella, head of family	12 Sep. 1873	C-221
O'Brien, John; Mary	18 Mar. 1863	A-545
O'Brien, Matthew, married	8 Dec. 1870	B-484
O'Brien, Nellie C., head of family; widowed sister; unmarried sister	29 May 1899	I-207
O'Callaghan, Maria A.; Richard	21 Sep. 1882	E-267
O'Connor, Ella; Robert	6 Nov. 1896	H-501
O'Connor, Peter, married	5 Mar. 1874	C-288
O'Donnell, Elizabeth; George W.; 1 child	8 Nov. 1915	L-227
O'Donovan, Mary; Bartholomew (E-83)	9 Nov. 1876	D-52
O'Elmore, Samuel; Mary Jane	9 Feb. 1861	A-120
Oettl, Augusta; Franz	11 Apr. 1876	C-509
O'Farrell, Jasper; Maria	22 Apr. 1862	A-460
Ogburn, Chas. E.; wife	3 Dec. 1894	H-116
Ogden, Andrew F.; single (F-559; G-202)	20 June 1883	E-345
O'Grady, Johanna; Thomas	24 Mar. 1873	C-129
O'Groman, Anna; Mathew	22 Nov. 1916	L-314
Ohrt, Adolf; family	19 Oct. 1878	D-344
Oldham, May Cleveland; Wm. G.; one son	26 Mar. 1915	L-155
O'Leary, Thomas; Bridgit (E-95; E-562)	30 Oct. 1878	D-347
Oliver, Alice G.; mother Mary A. Oliver, a widow	18 July 1918	L-415
Oliver, Jas. F., married	29 Sep. 1876	D-42
Oliver, Kate; J. S.	23 Jan. 1905	J-53
Olivera, Vitel Jose; wife; 11 children	16 June 1915	L-184
Ollis, Frank; Mamie; children:: Chester, Kenneth	28 Nov. 1908	K-188
Olmsted, O. A., married	31 July 1860	A-17
Oman, George W.; Melvina (C-395)	25 Apr. 1861	A-317
O'Neill, James, married	19 Oct. 1871	B-573
O'Neill, Jennie; head of family	10 Jan. 1896	H-353
Orender, Joel; wife	27 June 1878	D-277
Organ, Jennie; Thos H.	29 Jan. 1885	F-17
Ormsby, Clara J.; M. P. (abandonment filed 4/5/1883)	11 Sep. 1882	E-261
Ormsby, Elijah S., married	14 Jan. 1869	B-309
Ormsby, Jno. S.; Jane	1 Mar. 1861	A-152
Orr, Charlotte; Francis H.	31 Mar. 1913	K-495
Orr, T. L.; son Marshall C. Orr	20 Jan. 1919	L-455

Applicant and Family Information	Filing Date	Vol.-Pg.
Orth, Anna; Henry; probate	3 Aug. 1889	D-494
Ortman, Mrs. Kathrina; J. J.	31 Jan. 1911	K-364
Orzi, Ancilla; Rafaello	18 Dec. 1884	E-531
O'Shea, Wm., married	19 Apr. 1872	C-79
Oster, Henry; wife	17 Sep. 1900	I-293
Otis, Flora E., Hamilton	8 Nov. 1906	K-15
Ott, Mary S.; Raymond L.	30 Mar. 1916	L-267
Ottenfield, Katie Von, unmarried	9 Sep. 1919	L-494
Ottmer, M. I.; H. C., husband	11 July 1907	K-57
Overton, Wm. M.; wife	14 Feb. 1895	H-169
Owen, Emma; Charles A.	1 Dec. 1909	K-280
Owen, Mrs. F. F.; R. R.	9 Jan. 1889	F-528
Owen, Venia; Columbus W.	19 Aug. 1913	L-26
Owen, W. P.; Amanda I.	8 Feb. 1876	C-487

Applicant and Family Information	Filing Date	Vol.-Pg.
Paaskesen, Meller	31 Jan. 1917	L-328
Paine, John; Emeline A.	15 Apr. 1862	A-433
Paladini, A.; Teresa; 5 children	30 Mar. 1909	K-218
Palmer, Elias B., married	9 Aug. 1872	B-587
Palmer, Eliz. A.; C. H.	10 Jan. 1883	E-302
Palmer, Geo. B., married	2 Dec. 1868	B-282
Palmer, James M.	29 Oct. 1889	F-610
Palmer, Martha A., nee: Mardis; James Palmer	8 Mar. 1905	J-56
Palmer, Rebecca; Jasper C.	17 Apr. 1906	J-130
Palmer, Sophie L.; E. S., husband	28 Feb. 1910	K-300
Parasso, G. B.; wife	23 Sep. 1885	F-134
Pari, or Pear, L., married	24 Aug. 1877	C-595
Paris, Wilhelmine	8 Nov. 1917	L-381
Parish, Wm.; family	17 May 1885	E-472
Park, Ellen A.; Alvah W. (8/6/1883, E-360)	14 May 1880	D-571
Park, Geo. W.; Mary L.; probate	21 Dec. 1903	H-218
Park, Theo. T.; Lizzie C.	23 June 1879	D-427
Parker, Cynthia A.; Freeman	20 July 1875	D-25
Parker, Edwin C.; married; 2 children	23 Jan. 1878	D-205
Parker, E. D., married	14 May 1873	C-156
Parker, Eliza A.; Freeman	31 July 1879	D-443
Parker, Frances S.; J. C.	13 Mar. 1900	I-257
Parker, James; married	31 Oct. 1867	B-201
Parkerson, C. J.; wife	20 Dec. 1886	F-341
Parkinson, Chas. E.; Rosa L.; 1 child	28 July 1905	J-87
Parks, A. H.; wife	22 May 1885	F-55
Parr, Barbara; John	5 Feb. 1906	J-122
Parrish, David F.; wife	18 Aug. 1885	F-112
Parrish, Sarah E.; married	30 Oct. 1869	B-363
Parrish, Wm.; wife	20 July 1880	D-589
Parsons, John M., head of family; Mary M. (10/11/1906, K-6; 5/12/1913, K-504)	14 Aug. 1888	F-487
Parsons, Harriet M.; John M.	2 May 1899	I-201
Parsons, Mary (B Probate Book lost); probate	14 Jan. 1876	B-429
Parsons, Orren V.; Mary F.	27 Oct. 1911	K-396
Passarino, G.; Luvisa	12 July 1902	I-404
Pastor, H. E.; Nellie S.	18 Mar. 1908	K-112
Patten, Charles C.; Amelia	16 Dec. 1909	K-283

Applicant and Family Information	Filing Date	Vol.-Pg.
Patten, Louisa, Joseph; 7 children (4/23/1877, D-65)	24 June 1873	C-178
Patten, Penelope J.; Hugh	21 Mar. 1862	A-411
Patten, P. J.; Hugh (11/5/1867, B-202)	29 Oct. 1860	A-61
Patterson, A. S., married	16 June 1874	C-316
Patterson, Mary Bell; widow of Andrew; 6 children	2 July 1908	K-137
Patterson, Wm., married (2/29/1872, C-54)	30 Apr. 1870	B-399
Patterson, Wm., single	12 Aug. 1897	H-606
Patterson, William; Mary	1 Apr. 1878	D-241
Patton, Carrie L.; Wm. F.	26 Feb. 1902	I-378
Patton, Eliz. R.; G. W.	2 Jan. 1894	H-15
Patton, Mollie M.	23 Mar. 1916	L-265
Pauli, Mary F.	1 Apr. 1915	L-157
Pauw, Mary, married	17 Apr. 1872	C-77
Paxton, Jane M.; Blitz	29 Dec. 1904	J-49
Payne, Anna M.; Jefferson	14 Jan. 1911	K-360
Payne, Lottie Anna; Daniel H. (9/18/1919, M-3)	14 June 1898	I-87
Payne, Louis R.	19 Sep. 1914	L-103
Payran, Stephen; Jane	21 Nov. 1867	B-74
Peabody, B. F.	4 May 1916	L-276
Pease, George O.	12 Sep. 1916	L-304
Peatross, William W., married	14 Dec. 1877	D-182
Peck, John, Jr.; wife	26 Aug. 1885	F-115
Peck, Morris; Phoebe (1/11/1896, H-356, different parcel)	6 Sep. 1895	H-281
Peck, S. S.; wife	29 Oct. 1897	I-8
Peck, Sarah Adalad; George; 4 children	13 Dec. 1873	C-266
Peck, Thos. Morris, head of household; 2 minors	4 Nov. 1898	I-143
Peckelhoff, Henry; wife	15 Apr. 1896	H-401
Pedrotti, Clara	29 July 1913	L-16
Pedrotti, Luis; Annabella	4 Oct. 1904	J-37
Peery, Thos. E.; Sarah A.	8 July 1898	I-97
Peirce, Job; wife	23 Jan. 1885	E-543
Penfield, G. P.; Henrietta	11 Aug. 1913	L-20
Pennine, A. S.; Sarah S.	8 Feb. 1867	B-83
Peoples, Nathan; wife	17 Dec.1880	E-57
Pepin, Louis; Pauline	31 Aug. 1906	J-149
Perinoni, Esolina; Philip	15 Mar. 1902	I-381
Perkins, George R.; Mary Ann	28 Mar. 1861	A-180
Perkins, Louisa, married; 8 children	9 Dec. 1874	C-351

Applicant and Family Information	Filing Date	Vol.-Pg.
Perkinson, Ellen F.; J. E.	24 Oct. 1876	D-47
Perreira, Louisa; Libanno/LiBauno	19 Dec. 1889	E-611
Perry, A. F.; wife	17 Oct. 1887	F-421
Perry, Alice L.; H. R.	9 Nov. 1889	F-620
Perry, Antone; Phoebe A. (1/23/1911, K-363)	3 Dec. 1908	K-190
Perry, Frank; Mariana (4/2/1908, K-113)	27 Nov. 1891	G-274
Perry, James A.; wife	10 May 1886	F-259
Perry, Jane M., married	25 May 1882	E-221
Perry, John; wife	14 Dec. 1885	F-176
Perry, Joseph M., married	6 Oct. 1873	C-233
Perry, Joseph; Maria Philomena, wf.; minors Elsie, Josie, Harry, Isabella, Louise, Frank, Willie (1/6/1913, K-481)	31 Mar. 1906	J-129
Perry, Wm. H.; Margaret H.	3 Dec. 1868	B-287
Peter, Arethusa; Silas	21 May 1879	D-413
Peter, Theresa; Martin	2 Dec. 1901	I-367
Peters, J.; married	12 Mar. 1894	H-34
Peters, John T.; wife (insolvent debtor, 4/22/1886, F-248; 9/5/1885, F-125)	12 Mar. 1885	F-36
Peters, Jordan/Jourdan; Mary	24 Apr. 1861	A-326
Peters, W. S.; Jacob	8 Sep. 1877	D-135
Peterson, Anna Marie; Andrew W. (11/11/1903, I-483)	11 July 1894	H-76
Peterson, Edwin; wife; 5 children	25 Aug. 1877	C-591
Peterson, G. H.; Ellen (11/3/1871, B-577; 3/3/1872, C-58)	7 Apr. 1862	A-424
Peterson, Meta A.	7 Jan. 1918	L-392
Peterson, Nels; wife	21 Jan. 1902	I-376
Peterson, Pelina A.; A.	14 Aug. 1894	H-89
Petit, Alexander P.; Catherine L.	9 Dec. 1867	B-174
Petit, Henriette; Jacques, dec'd (12/24/1888, D-471, probate)	29 Apr. 1881	E-92
Petray, Hattie M.; James A.	27 Oct. 1906	K-10
Petray, Mary L.; George W., dec'd	7 Nov. 1906	K-14
Petrie, Minnie E.	25 Mar. 1918	L-402
Petry, Ida; Joseph	26 Sep. 1904	J-33
Peugh, Christiana A.; James A. (28 Sep. 1876, D-40)	3 Aug. 1878	B-676
Pflying, Matilda; George (5/23/1888, F-469)	28 Oct. 1878	D-345
Phelps, Adna, married	13 May 1871	B-519
Philbee, James; Sarah J.	29 July 1882	E-251
Philbrook, D. C.; Emma Jane; 3 children	9 Oct. 1905	J-100
Philips, Eliza; John	16 May 1871	B-521
Philips, Lula J.; Frank C.; 2 children	18 July 1907	K-60

Applicant and Family Information	Filing Date	Vol.-Pg.
Philips, Nancy M.; P. J.; probate	27 Oct. 1891	E-236
Phillips, Jacob; married	18 Oct. 1875	C-445
Phillips, Sarah D.; Charles	14 July 1875	C-421
Philpott, Isabella; Thos. Henry (5/20/1918, L-409)	4 Sep. 1917	L-367
Philpott, Mary L.; husband J. F.; probate	25 Mar. 1895	F-251
Phinney, M. E.; Mrs.L.	22 Dec. 1890	G-148
Phinney, Ollean; Charley	16 Dec. 1907	K-86
Piatt, Eliza C.; Joseph P.	2 Oct. 1889	F-517
Picchi, Teresa; Pietro	20 July 1910	K-328
Pickering, Emma J.; Charles E.	20 Mar. 1907	K-36
Pickett, Wm.; Catherine B.	3 July 1871	B-547
Pierce, John K.; Helen Maria; 3 children (9/3/1907, K-70)	7 Oct. 1893	H-1
Pierucci, Marcello; Alaide	2 Sep. 1890	G-105
Pilastre, Elisa; Emile	28 Sep. 1903	I-474
Pippin, T. C.; wife	27 Dec. 1884	E-534
Pippin, Thos. C.; married	22 Apr. 1878	D-254
Pitt, J. W.; wife	2 Feb. 1886	F-217
Pitt, Wm. Ralph; wife; 6 children	7 July 1905	J-84
Pittroff, Harry C.	3 Mar. 1915	L-149
Pitts, Henry A.; wife	2 Sep. 1880	E-32
Pixley, Olive; James	17 Sep. 1901	I-354
Pleasant, Mary O.; George W.	14 Aug. 1908	K-156
Plunket, Eleanor; widow	2 Dec. 1889	E-605
Poff, Cordelia Lillian; Anthony	7 Mar. 1908	K-106
Poggie, Nannie J.; Frank	11 Jan. 1886	F-198
Pohley, Henry; Mary	11 Aug. 1875	C-430
Pohley, Joseph; married	3 July 1867	B-130
Polk, Charles E.; Josephine	19 May 1874	B-645
Polliner, Angelina; Francisco	6 Aug. 1903	I-459
Pomeroy, Lena M.; Campbell	10 Jan. 1921	M-67
Pometta, V. M.; Victoria C.; 2 children	15 June 1908	K-132
Pond, Freida F.; C. H.	15 Sep. 1898	I-120
Ponzo, Margherita; Chiafredo	3 Sep. 1918	L-427
Pool, Charles A.; Nellie E.	29 Nov. 1909	K-279
Pool, Jessie E.; Wm. H.	17 Mar. 1919	L-464
Pool, John, married; 5 children	11 Oct. 1877	D-149
Pool, Lydia; John, dec'd. (Deeds Book 76; page 70)	16 May 1881	
Poole, David; wife	3 Sep. 1881	E-135

Applicant and Family Information	Filing Date	Vol.-Pg.
Poole, William W.	29 Jan. 1915	L-138
Poppe, J. A., married (notarized July 25)	23 July 1860	A-13
Porcher, C. P.; Mary Elizabeth (5/19/1901, I-328; 7/17/1903, I-456; 8/13/1904, J-26)	13 Mar. 1897	H-557
Porter, Ann; Thomas	6 June 1885	F-69
Porter, Chas. J.; Nettie J.	26 Feb. 1894	H-27
Porter, Frank C.; Mary C.	29 Jan. 1861	A-115
Porter, H. M.; Annice/Annico (8/12/1872, B-590)	9 Aug. 1876	C-545
Porter, Mabel A.; J. F.	30 Oct. 1911	K-397
Porter, Rose M., widow; 2 children: Oscar, 5 yrs; Edward, 4 yrs.	11 May 1908	K-122
Porter, Wm. W.; wife	31 Aug. 1878	D-314
Porterfield, Bessie Marie; William H.	10 Jan. 1912	K-408
Porterfield, J. W.; Elizabeth J. (Abandonment 5/15/1877, A-273)	26 Dec. 1870	B-479
Potter, Jas. H.	30 Mar. 1915	L-156
Potter, Thos. P.; wife	28 Sep. 1891	G-237
Potter, William R.	30 Mar. 1915	L-156
Pottle, B. N., married	16 June 1877	C-559
Potts, Ella; Thos. A.	30 June 1898	I-93
Poulson, Mary; Fred C.	30 Dec. 1908	K-195
Poulson, Mary	18 Jan. 1915	L-134
Poulterer, Mina C.; Thomas J.	28 Oct. 1872	C-123
Powell, Katie Irene; Jesse Rausom, dec'd's father; no children; probate	19 Jan. 1903	H-131
Powell, R.; wife	26 Feb. 1885	F-27
Power, Catharine; Wm. I.	13 Nov. 1868	B-276
Powers, Chas. C.; wife	18 Sep. 1884	E-511
Powers, David; wife	16 Feb. 1888	F-455
Powers, David P.; Mary C.	2 July 1867	B-126
Powers, Frank E.; wife	21 July 1899	I-210
Powers, Jane; Jess	22 June 1882	E-234
Powers, Jane; Jessie	28 July 1892	G-330
Powell, Mary M.; Ransom	22 July 1862	A-499
Pratt, Eugene F.; wife	5 Dec. 1885	E-552
Pressey, Daniel G.; married	21 July 1877	C-577
Pressley, John G.; wife	30 Apr. 1879	D-406
Prestiss, Ella E.; Arthur O., dec'd; minors: Don C.; Archie D.	12 Mar. 1907	K-24
Preston, Bessie; Wm. H.	4 Jan. 1906	J-117

Applicant and Family Information	Filing Date	Vol.-Pg.
Preston, H. L.; Emily	20 June 1876	C-668
Prewett, Mary, widow of John	18 Mar. 1864	A-594
Price, Andrew; wife	6 May 1882	E-214
Price, J. K.; no family	5 Apr. 1880	D-547
Priest, Martha	9 Nov. 1914	L-111
Prince, Peter; wife	14 June 1882	E-231
Prince, Thos. R.; Abigail S.	24 Apr. 1861	A-284
Pritchitt, Eliz.; James	26 Dec. 1883	E-409
Pritchett, G. S.; Ida	27 Feb. 1908	K-101
Pritchett, Laura Belle; A. W.	26 Jan. 1920	M-19
Proctor, Catherine; Ira	6 Jan. 1882	E-176
Proctor, C. B., married	8 June 1870	B-413
Proctor, Sadie R.; Royal T.	12 Aug. 1908	K-153
Proctor, Sarah Jane; Charles E.	26 Oct. 1885	F-146
Proctor, T. W.; wife	24 Feb. 1885	F-24
Proctor, Verlander C.; husband David D. (abandonment 12/6/1906)	5 Mar. 1887	F-365
Provines, Alexander P.; Cornelia Bissell	7 June 1879	D-424
Prows, Daniel, married	8 Apr. 1868	B-219
Prows, Sylvester W.; Eliz.; (2/27/1890, G-18; 6/6/1896, H-436; 7/18/1885, F-97)	8 Dec. 1870	B-471
Puckett, Mary C.; Edward H.	22 May 1871	B-525
Purrington, Joseph; Frances (9/27/1894, G-501)	21 Aug. 1861	A-376
Purrington, Louisa M.	14 Dec. 1915	L-241
Purser, Edward T.; Ann	12 Aug. 1901	I-348
Purvine, Walter F.; wife	29 Nov. 1887	F-431
Putnam, D. W. C.; wf. R. A.	8 June 1866	A-704
Pyatt, Thomas H.; wife Artemetia	29 Oct. 1860	A-63

Applicant and Family Information	Filing Date	Vol.-Pg.
Quackenbush, Robert P.; wife (10/16/1877, D-165)	30 Jan. 1880	D-509
Quackenbush, Sarah Ann; U. P.	28 Feb. 1895	H-174
Quackenbush, Uriah P., married	10 Sep. 1867	B-142
Quigly, B. H.; Delilah	24 Apr. 1861	A-265
Quinlan, Albert G., married	10 May 1872	C-93
Quinlan, John, married	1 Mar. 1877	D-95
Quinn, Annie; P.	15 Aug. 1890	G-89
Quinn, Catharine, married	21 Mar. 1874	C-294
Quinn, John; Margaret (E-205)	1 Feb. 1881	E-70
Quinn, Margaret; John	30 May 1879	D-420
(von) Quitzow, Albert; Amelia	2 June 1870	B-410

Applicant and Family Information	Filing Date	Vol.-Pg.
Rackliff, Julia M.; Eugene L.	20 Dec. 1909	K-284
Rafael, Manuel Ignacio; wf. Ignacio Rose; no children; probate	7 Jan. 1896	F-373
Rafael, Pulisenia/Polcena; M. E. (I-432) (7/8/1908, K-143)	1 Feb. 1896	H-380
Railsback, Wm. H.; Mary Jane (10/12/1870, B-458)	11 Apr. 1861	A-214
Rainey, A. C.; Martha N. (B-163)	19 Nov. 1866	B-67
Rains, Agnes; Gallant (I-295; I-258)	30 July 1888	F-480
Rains, W. P.; no family mentioned	25 June 1889	F-589
Ralston, Annie; John	23 Feb. 1877	D-86
Rambo, Ann; widow of Isaac	9 Feb. 1861	A-127
Ramoni, Cora Walker; F. L.	1 Mar. 1915	L-148
Ramos, Carolina E.; Jose C.	14 Dec. 1897	I-26
Rand, Joseph; Marian W.	6 May 1865	A-648
Randall, Raymond L.; Hattie F.	28 May 1913	L-3
Randolph, E. B.; Rosa	11 Aug. 1913	L-21
Randolph, Eliza; Orton	6 July 1867	B-129
Randolph, Rachael C., widow	23 Apr. 1861	A-301
Rapun, Angel; wife	10 Mar. 1897	H-553
Rasmason, Peter; wife	20 Nov. 1886	F-329
Rasmussen, Eva; A.	4 Sep. 1913	L-28
Rathbun, Edwin D., married	11 Aug. 1870	B-443
Rathbun, Erskine; Cynthia M.	27 Mar. 1861	A-177
Ray, Elvira, married	10 July 1865	A-660
Raymond, Helen A.; Charles F. (F-352)	19 Sep. 1878	D-327
Raynaud, Paul B.; Ella H.; 2 children	9 Nov. 1906	K-17
Rea, Martha Ann, widow	3 Aug. 1903	I-458
Read, Robert; wife	9 July 1884	E-483
Reagan, John; married	17 May 1876	D-29
Redmond, Mrs. Jane; Patrick	21 Sep. 1885	F-132
Reed, Bridget; Michael	14 Dec. 1885	F-177
Reed, Daisy T.; Clarence E.	15 Aug. 1898	I-104
Reed, Emeline, unmarried	24 Apr. 1861	A-343
Reed, James F., married	20 Apr. 1871	B-512
Reed, Margaret; Joseph H.	10 Apr. 1889	F-552
Rees, C. W., married	14 Mar. 1861	A-161
Regan, John, married (C-520)	21 May 1872	C-101
Rego, Victorina Gloria, widow; minor dau. Adelaide	16 Apr. 1919	L-467
Rehe, Alma; Chas.	17 Aug. 1917	L-363
Reichenbach, Grace Anna; Magnus F. (6/23/1890, D-566,	29 Oct. 1885	F-150

Applicant and Family Information	Filing Date	Vol.-Pg.
probate)		
Reid, Sarah R. Cobb; Nelson B.	24 Apr. 1918	L-407
Remer, Mrs. Lida; Eugene B.	18 Mar. 1912	K-418
Remley, Mildred C.; widow of Wm.;(minor children: Wm., Leona, Mildred, Carrie	10 Sep. 1898	I-118
Renfro, S. W.; family	24 Sep. 1878	D-330
Renstrom, Ole; Hulda	13 Mar. 1911	K-369
Respini, Giovani; wife	23 Nov. 1896	H-507
Reyburn, L. C., married	24 Apr. 1861	A-323
Reynolds, John W., married	26 Feb. 1866	A-696
Reynolds, O. M.; W. D., husband	1 May 1916	L-275
Reynolds, William J.; I. Sabelle	3 Sep. 1860	A-22
Rhoades, Daniel; Mary Ann	15 Apr. 1863	A-549
Rhoades, Joan; Sam'l	31 Mar. 1894	H-43
Riblet, H. M.; Alma	15 Dec. 1919	M-14
Rice, Caroline E., widow; family	2 Jan. 1879	D-371
Rice, Eliza Ann; Patrick (B-529)	18 Sep. 1869	B-349
Rich, J. P.; Sarah S.	22 Oct. 1863	A-567
Rich, Wm. B.; Ella	21 July 1896	H-461
Richards, Edwin; Bessie	9 Mar. 1916	L-259
Richards, Philena H.; John, dec'd; probate	22 Oct. 1898	G-240
Richardson, Clifton P.; Gertrude Sands; children: Dorothy, Kathleen	6 July 1915	L-190
Richardson, Eliza C.; Forrest C.	24 Jan. 1910	K-288
Richardson, Evalena V.; husband M.	11 Nov. 1908	K-182
Richardson, Margaret; James	15 May 1865	A-650
Richardson, Walter M.; Jessie G.	8 May 1915	L-172
Richman, Louis P.; Jane A.; no children	29 June 1909	K-238
Rickard, J. S.; married	10 May 1867	B-108
Ricklifs, Alice B.; Peter H. (L-159)	8 May 1896	H-408
Ricklifs, Alice L.; Henry H.	11 July 1893	G-432
Ricksecker, Henriette E.; Lucius E.	22 Jan. 1895	H-139
Riddle, David M.; Susan M. (I-316; I-363)	10 Jan. 1893	G-392
Ridenhour, Lewis W.; Mary E.	16 Apr. 1861	A-230
Rider, Lewis E.; Susie E.	29 Feb. 1916	L-256
Riedi, Valentine; wife	16 Mar. 1900	I-259
Rien, Samuel; wife	14 June 1878	D-270
Riens, Wm.; Abbie	23 June 1877	C-562
Riese, Ada; Herman	5 Dec. 1898	I-157

Applicant and Family Information	Filing Date	Vol.-Pg.
Riewertz, Henry M.; Mathilde; 4 min. children: Ocke, Christ, Minnie, Mattie; probate	8 Oct. 1895	F-328
Riley, Catherine; Patrick	14 Nov. 1892	G-373
Rippeto, O.; married to …Pattow	28 Apr. 1862	A-482
Rippin, Mary A.; Wm.	2 Mar. 1917	L-336
Risdon, Sarah T., married	16 Mar. 1878	D-237
Risso, G. B.; Maria; 3 children	30 Mar. 1909	K-217
Ritchie, Mary Agnes; James Taylor	10 Oct. 1903	I-477
Ritchie, James Taylor; wife	22 Oct. 1903	I-481
Ritter, Mary E.; Carl E.	27 Jan. 1909	K-201
Rizzi, Luigi; Virginia	29 Oct. 1913	L-38
Roach, Thomas; Anna (12/6/1876; D-57)	15 May 1873	C-137
Robbins, A. S., wife of George; 6 children	11 Mar. 1886	F-240
Roberson, Jas. Edward; wife	28 Dec. 1899	I-234
Roberts, Charles; wife	24 Mar. 1890	G-30
Roberts, Edward W., married	17 Feb. 1877	D-83
Roberts, Mrs. Elizabeth G.; Charles	20 Aug. 1887	F-407
Roberts, Eliz.; Robert E. (3/1/1895, H-177)	23 Mar. 1889	F-541
Roberts, Mrs. Emily H., widow; 7 children	9 May 1899	I-203
Roberts, John M.; wife	29 Jan. 1886	F-209
Roberts, Inez M.; husband James M.	24 July 1907	K-61
Roberts, J. S., married	4 Oct. 1870	B-456
Roberts, Mary, single	8 Apr. 1882	E-204
Robertson, A. B.; wife	28 Sep. 1903	J-34
Robertson, Henry A.; Miney	16 June 1876	C-530
Robertson, Mary; John W.	26 Aug. 1897	H-621
Robertson, Robert; Phebe S.	5 Apr. 1861	A-187
Robertson, Sarah A., married (Robinson)	14 June 1865	A-652
Robertson, W. D.; unmarried; 1 child	26 Oct. 1906	K-9
Robinson, Fanny J.; B. K.	18 Jan. 1878	D-202
Robinson, Mary; J. R.	20 July 1880	D-591
Robinson, Sarah M.; John W. (D-5)	16 Oct. 1874	C-336
Robinson, S. S., married	24 May 1873	C-162
Robinson, W. I.; Abigail M.	10 June 1910	K-324
Robison, Caroline, widow	8 Mar. 1886	F-238
Roche, Joseph T.; Alice P.	19 Nov. 1917	L-384
Rochford, Thos.; Sebina L.; family (A-68; C-367)	22 Jan. 1879	D-375
Rockhold, S. N., married	25 Jan. 1877	D-77

Applicant and Family Information	Filing Date	Vol.-Pg.
Rodd, Mary J.; Samuel (I-369)	28 Nov. 1892	G-375
Rodeck, Letitia; John	20 Sep. 1872	D-3
Rodehaver, Amelia C.; John P. (7/15/1879, D-433; F-186)	13 June 1878	D-265
Rodgers, A. W., married	29 June 1868	B-246
Rodgers, Frances Jeanette; John	5 July 1884	E-479
Rodgers, Ida; Robt. F.	13 July 1896	H-450
Rodgers, John; Ann	17 Dec. 1862	A-523
Rodgers, Nancy E.; Warren	26 Sep. 1899	I-218
Roe, Teresa Fink; Chas. C.	6 Feb. 1915	L-144
Roe, Wm. S.; family	18 Sep. 1879	D-465
Rogers, Alexander W.; Mary Ann	6 Mar. 1861	A-149
Rogers, Harriet L., married	11 July 1872	C-122
Rogers, Lucinda M., head of family; minors: 7	25 Nov. 1898	I-151
Rogers, W. K.; wife	18 Aug. 1892	G-338
Rohr, Rosalie C.; S. M., husband	3 June 1912	K-427
Rohrer, Calvin; Susan	17 Nov. 1860	A-141
Rollins, Harriet F.; Calvin I.	29 July 1915	L-199
Rommell, Mary Alice; Geo. B.	8 June 1901	I-335
Roney, J. M., married	15 May 1877	D-128
Roof, George M.; Matilda	7 Mar. 1916	L-258
Rose, B. N.; Dale M.	21 Apr. 1920	M-29
Rose, J. W., married	19 Dec. 1874	C-356
Rose, Mary; Jerry; minor children: Jerry, William, Charles, Lena	15 Feb. 1921	M-74
Rose, Rufus C.; wife	28 July 1884	E-489
Rosenberg, Esther C.; Wolf	2 Jan. 1890	E-615
Rosenberg, Jeremiah W., married	22 Jan. 1868	B-205
Rosenberg, John, married	18 Sep. 1869	B-350
Rosenthal, Joseph, married	24 Dec. 1872	D-17
Ross, Mrs. Ellen; Gilbert McM.	7 Jan. 1886	F-194
Ross, Mrs. Harriett M.; William D.	4 Oct. 1907	K-76
Ross, Lena; George A.	21 Aug. 1908	K-157
Ross, Martha A.; H. J.	9 Apr. 1897	H-571
Ross, Mary E.; hus. Kemp L. dec:d, (K-307); Milton Kemp, minor	12 July 1905	J-85
Ross, Milburn, married	21 Dec. 1874	C-359
Ross, Ridley B., Eviza Ann	19 Dec. 1874	C-357
Ross, Robert, married	14 May 1878	B-674
Ross, William; Elizabeth Mehegan	3 Jan. 1863	A-528

Applicant and Family Information	Filing Date	Vol.-Pg.
Rossi, Antonio; wife	30 Dec. 1903	I-488
Rotchford, Thomas, married	21 Jan. 1876	C-480
Roth, Fritz; Frances	10 Nov. 1914	L-113
Rotthaus, Anna Emily; F.	17 Aug. 1915	L-205
Rovai, Louise; F. P.	8 Jan. 1903	I-426
Rowe, Nicholas; family	27 Sep. 1881	E-139
Rowland, Minnie C.; E. S.	4 Dec. 1908	K-192
Rowlson, Eliza A.; E. E.	28 Oct. 1895	H-307
Royal, Helen A.	27 June 1876	B-670
Rude, Thos. G., married (D-290)	4 Apr. 1878	D-242
Rudesiel, Jessie P.; family	4 Oct. 1861	A-382
Rudesiel, John A.; Sarah J.	26 Aug. 1861	A-377
Ruffner, Charles K.; unmarried (L-279)	17 Apr. 1915	L-165
Rugg, Emily Jane; John T. (4/29/1868, B-231)	27 Nov. 1866	B-69
Rugg, Fannie A.; W. H.	18 Apr. 1888	F-463
Runnison/Rennison, Margaret, married	9 Oct. 1871	B-567
Runyon, Robt. B.; Julia Ann	1 Oct. 1883	E-385
Runyon, Sarah M.; Wm. S.	9 Oct. 1917	L-374
Rupe, David C., unmarried	26 Dec. 1870	B-477
Rupe, Samuel H.; Margaret J. (A-517; abandonment A-93)	26 Dec. 1860	A-93
Russell, A. W.; Henrie H., wife	6 Oct. 1860	A-38
Russell, Edna E.; Clarence J.	27 July 1917	L-361
Russell, Hugh A.; Sarah	19 Apr. 1861	A-255
Russell, Laura Frances; Geo. W.	26 Jan. 1917	L-327
Rutherford, John; Katherine; no children	9 Mar. 1912	K-416
Rutledge, Adelaide M.; Thomas	3 Sep. 1892	G-342
Ryan, P.; wife	5 Aug. 1884	E-492
Ryan, Patrick H., married	11 Aug. 1869	B-343
Ryan, W. H., married	13 Jan. 1875	C-365

Applicant and Family Information	Filing Date	Vol.-Pg.
Sackett, David A.; Emily I. (A-370, 402, 495, 547)	30 July 1860	A-9
Sadlo, M.; wife	12 June 1886	F-271
Sammons, Emma E.; Harvey	23 Mar. 1915	L-154
Samuels, James; Sarah	23 Apr. 1861	A-319
Samuels, Jessie M.; James M.	12 Apr. 1912	K-421
Samuels, Uriah, married	12 Oct. 1874	C-335
Sanborn, Mrs. Emma Rose; W. B.	2 Feb. 1890	G-7
Sanborn, Ezra T.; Cordelia G.	19 Feb. 1864	A-589
Sanborn, G. N.; Emily J.	18 May 1866	B-14
Sanborn, J. Adelaide S.; Geo. P.	8 Feb. 1917	L-331
Sansom, Elias, married; widower; 1 child (11/14/1866, B-57) (A-151)	19 Sep. 1860	A-26
Santos, J.; wife, Virginia; 6 minors	4 Sep. 1917	L-368
Sapwell, James; Minnie B.; no children	15 July 1912	K-437
Sargent, Henry, married	15 May 1867	B-109
Sarginsson, Cornelius; Sophia; 3 children	21 Mar. 1913	K-493
Sartori, Mary; John	19 Dec. 1918	L-450
Satterwhite, W. C., not married	16 Oct. 1912	K-462
Saul, Geo. M.; May Catherine	8 Feb. 1883	E-437
Saum, Cordelia H.; Geo.	18 Aug. 1883	E-366
Saunders, William Wallace; Jessie; sons Wallace, Ernest	1 Feb. 1917	L-329
Savage, G. N., married (E-180)	25 Feb. 1876	C-498
Sawyer, Lucy H., widow	16 Apr. 1884	E-459
Saxton, Fred L.; Carrie; 5 children (minors)	21 Oct. 1918	L-442
Scales, Jane E., married	30 Dec. 1873	C-272
Scammon, Charles M.; Susan C.	12 May 1876	C-517
Scannell, Jeremiah, married; Hannah (D-90)	26 May 1874	B-650
Schaefer, August; Otilde; 4 children (Bankrupt 3/6/1917, Promiscuous File M-208	23 Sep. 1912	K-452
Schaefer, Mrs. Cecilia; Ignatz (C-303)	12 Dec. 1885	F-173
Schafer, Sarah Cecilia; Ignatz (F-465, probate)	14 July 1886	F-286
Schell, Margaret L.; Frederick A.	11 Oct. 1909	K-272
Scherrer, Mathilda; Jacob dec'd 3/29/1905; minor: Frederick C.	9 Nov. 1905	J-105
Schetter, Elizabeth J.; Otto	10 June 1893	G-426
Schevo, Clara; James	14 Mar. 1877	D-98
Schiapacasse, Antonio; Mary Angela	31 May 1861	A-365
Schieck, Margartha Agnes; Johan Gottried dec'd; probate, David Schieck, exec.	25 Apr. 1901	G-582

Applicant and Family Information	Filing Date	Vol.-Pg.
Schieffer, Della A.; William H.	13 Mar. 1917	L-339
Schendel, John; Anna	27 Aug. 1872	B-595
Schilling, Susanna; J. A.	10 Dec. 1917	L-387
Schleth, Mary; William, minor; husband D. F. dec'd	13 May 1910	K-320
Schlunegger, Christian; Mary	7 Sep. 1909	K-257
Schluter, Florence E.; W. E.	21 Dec. 1908	K-194
Schmesar, Ross A.; Albert C.	27 June 1902	I-399
Schmiedeskamp, A. J.; Amanda M.; 2 children	7 Aug. 1918	L-424
Schmidt, Mary Delphine Blanche; John	24 July 1916	L-294
Schmidt, V.; wife (H-242; 10/8/1895, F-331, probate)	22 Jan. 1891	G-161
Schmitt, Mary; Geo. (I-405)	29 Jan. 1894	H-22
Schott, John; wife; 3 children.	29 Nov. 1873	C-259
Schourp, Otto R.; Sadie I.; no children	10 Feb. 1913	K-486
Schuler, C. O., married, head of family	7 Apr. 1880	G-33
Schulte, H. F., married	20 Dec. 1873	C-237
Schultz, Edward, married	25 Jan. 1877	C-560
Schumacher, E. F.; Alice	24 Nov. 1874	C-346
Schumacher, Peter J.; Martha (L-293)	14 Nov. 1900	I-304
Schwan, Leonard; wife	6 May 1873	C-151
Scofield, Franklin A., married	17 Sep. 1877	D-148
Scott, Barbara E., married	3 June 1868	B-238
Scott, Betsey; James	5 Nov. 1862	A-515
Scott, Eli; Martha E.; minor	25 May 1907	K-44
Scott, Elizabeth; D. P. H.	15 Mar. 1880	G-32
Scott, Malinda; husband; 11 children	29 Nov. 1886	F-331
Scott, Mary E.; Julius (G-443)	24 Mar. 1893	G-402
Scott, Milton; wife	5 Aug. 1895	H-253
Scott, Mrs. Sarah A.; Wm. T.	1 Feb. 1895	H-154
Scott, Mrs. S. W.; W.	26 June 1885	F-82
Scott, Stewart; unmarried; maintains mother	25 Oct. 1898	I-139
Scott, Wm. A., married	2 Mar. 1867	B-92
Scudder, Jacob C.; Nancy D. (C-374; F-41)	13 Oct. 1869	B-357
Seaman, Mrs. C. J.; Murvin Burnhardt	18 June 1906	J-138
Seaman, Lena S.; J. A.	9 Aug. 1880	E-27
Sears, Franklin; Margaret	13 Jan. 1864	A-581
Sears, G. C. P.; wife	12 Sep. 1889	E-581
Seawell, Wm. N., married	8 July 1876	D-32
Sebring, Thomas; Margaret E.	18 Mar. 1867	B-97
Sedgley, Jotham; Mary P. (D-485)	18 Nov. 1864	A-624

Applicant and Family Information	Filing Date	Vol.-Pg.
Seiaroni, Lucy; Peter	8 Dec. 1913	L-44
Seid, Morris; Eva	12 Mar. 1917	L-338
Seipel, Daisy L.; N. A.	9 Aug. 1913	L-19
Seipp, John C.; Maria E.	26 July 1870	B-433
Semel, William; Mary; 3 children (I-15; L-110)	28 May 1912	K-425
Service, Charles A., widower; 2 minor daughters	30 Nov. 1920	M-61
Seversen, Charles E.; Ida	29 Dec. 1914	L-126
Shaefer, Adeline; Otto H.; Adeline's daughter	13 Sep. 1912	K-447
Shafer, Eliz. G.; John S.	22 Jan. 1880	D-507
Shafer, George, widower	15 Jan. 1866	A-690
Shafer, John N.; wife; 1 grandchildren	11 Feb. 1897	H-537
Shaffer, Alice A.; Wm. J.	19 Aug. 1913	L-25
Shaffer, Emily M.; Reuben H., Sr.; children Calvin, Earl C. & Fern R.	16 Apr. 1914	L-76
Sharkey, John H.; Louisa; no children	31 July 1918	L-422
Sharp, Amelia; David	4 Apr. 1900	I-267
Sharp, Charles, married	29 Jan. 1877	D-79
Shattuck, David; Elizabeth A. (A-287; B-342)	8 Apr. 1861	A-206
Shattuck, Dickson P.; Nancy	18 Apr. 1861	A-292
Shattuck, Gilbert; Hannah L.	8 Aug. 1870	B-439
Shaver, Nancy; husband	18 May 1880	D-576
Shaw, Lovina R.; F. D. C., husband; child, Lydon M., probate	6 Dec. 1892	E-432
Shaw, Thomas A., married	27 July 1870	B-432
Shearer, Wm. P.; Pocahontas	14 Aug. 1903	I-463
Shedd, E. D. (male); family of 2 children	6 Nov. 1882	E-281
Shedd, M. R. J.; E. D.	7 May 1885	F-49
Sheehy, Hannah; Chs.	7 Dec. 1888	F-521
Shelford, Ida L.; husband	21 Jan. 1902	I-375
Shepard, Wm. P.; Mrs. Mary E.	16 May 1902	I-392
Shepherd, Alexander; Clementine M.	24 Nov. 1860	A-65
Sheplar, Louise E.; Sam. H.	7 Dec. 1891	G-283
Sherburne, E. R., unmarried	19 Mar. 1874	C-293
Sherman, Mrs. Rosalia; Daniel	18 July 1894	H-81
Sherry, Margaret; Thos.	24 Jan. 1874	C-279
Shipley, R. J.; Mary Ann	22 Apr. 1862	A-458
Shirley, Almira C.; James Q.	25 Apr. 1861	A-352
Shores, Leander/Lander, married	29 Jan. 1868	B-203
Short, Moses S.; Margaret	19 Apr. 1861	A-250
Schultz/Scoults, Martha Ann, married	25 Nov. 1870	B-466

Applicant and Family Information	Filing Date	Vol.-Pg.
Show, A. J.; Mrs. G. I.	19 Oct. 1897	I-5
Shriver, Addie M.; James B.	1 Oct. 1912	K-454
Shuler, Sarah Ann Leah; Geo.	13 Mar. 1885	F-38
Shull, S. M., married	28 July 1871	B-563
Shulte, Margaret E.; Wm. H.	22 May 1905	J-74
Shulte, Mary E., married	21 July 1875	D-27
Shultz, David J.; Martha (5/10/1869; B-329)	16 Apr. 1862	A-438
Shuster, J. E.; mother Sarah E.	24 Sep. 1902	I-417
Shuster, J.; mother; 2 sisters	23 Feb. 1894	H-25
Sibillia, Maria; Pietro	20 Aug. 1915	L-207
Sichrist, Chas. D.; Elizabeth	1 May 1861	A-283
Sickles, Nellie A.; Joseph E.	1 Sep. 1884	E-506
Sicotte, Ferdinand, married (Dec'd 9/20/1895, F-311, probate, G-178)	25 Sep. 1876	D-38
Siegel, Valentine; Minnie A. (8/13/1873, C-215)	20 Oct. 1868	B-271
Siegrist, Theresa; Peter (see abandonment)	21 Mar. 1911	K-373
Sill, Carrie; J. L., husband; 1 child	3 Feb. 1912	K-413
Silsby, H. W.; Eudora M.	18 Aug. 1891	G-217
Silva, A. B.; Bisenca	2 Dec. 1901	I-366
Silva, Flomania; M. G.	18 Mar. 1895	H-192
Silva, John J.; wife	31 Jan. 1896	H-377
Silva, Jose S.; wife	4 Dec. 1891	G-277
Silva, Manuel G.; wife	26 June 1880	D-585
Silva, M. G., head of family	3 Mar. 1880	D-535
Silva, Rufus J., widower; minor children: Raymond, Miriam, Beatrice	18 Nov. 1919	M-13
Silver, Henrietta A., widow	15 June 1874	C-314
Silvera, Maria; John	28 Aug. 1895	H-267
Silvia, John Jos.; wife	31 Jan. 1899	I-213
Silvia, Joseph D.; Mary S.	2 July 1874	B-652
Simmonds, Evelyn J.; Louis A.	23 Jan. 1907	K-29
Simmons, Alonzo; Jennette	29 Sep. 1877	D-155
Simmons, Emma; Joseph C. A.	4 Jan. 1892	G-289
Simmons, John P.; wife	5 Feb. 1885	F-20
Simmons, J. R.; wife	19 July 1882	E-246
Simmons, Margie; James S.	3 Nov. 1898	I-141
Simoni, Anna; Louis	21 Dec. 1892	G-388
Simons, Marie; Joseph	17 Apr. 1901	I-322
Simons, John S., married	4 Sep. 1874	C-325

Applicant and Family Information	Filing Date	Vol.-Pg.
Simons, W. H.; wife	16 May 1904	J-15
Simonson, O. M.; Josie E.; 3 minors	27 Feb. 1919	L-463
Simonton, Mrs. Ida N.; Charles E. (E-488)	21 July 1883	E-355
Simonton, William B., married	20 May 1875	C-402
Simpson, Margaret A.; formerly Margaret A. Dalzell, married	14 July 1866	B-26
Simpson, Wm.; Sarah (abandonments)	12 Dec. 1860	A-76
Sims, John; wife	12 May 1879	D-410
Sims, Katharine, married	17 July 1867	B-131
Singley, James, married	24 Apr. 1861	A-298
Sink, Mariette F.; Wm. O.	6 Sep. 1894	J-490
Skarratt, Carleton F.; Luella; 3 children	9 Apr. 1913	K-497
Skellenger, D. A.; Sopha/Sophia	4 May 1881	E-90
Skillman, Andrew; Jane (A-513)	22 Dec. 1860	A-81
Skillman, Theodore; wife; minor George Van Nest Skillman	21 Oct. 1907	K-79
Skinner, B. R., married	17 May 1871	B-523
Skinner, Helen M.; Rich M. (I-362)	1 Sep. 1897	H-627
Skinner, Rebecca T.; widow	23 July 1901	I-344
Slater, Jennie M.; Francis M.	9 Mar. 1908	K-107
Slattery, Louise W.; John J.	5 Jan. 1915	L-129
Slaven, Hannah H.; James	13 May 1868	B-234
Slocum, Geo.; wife	1 Mar. 1890	G-20
Sloper, Willard, head of family	24 Feb. 1880	D-531
Smalley, Simeon; no mention of marriage or family	17 Apr. 1861	A-239
Smith, Abbie L.; Jay H.	8 Nov. 1912	K-467
Smith, Adam; wife	10 July 1891	G-199
Smith, Alexander H., married	16 Jan. 1877	D-73
Smith, Alfred Wm.; wife	11 Nov. 1885	F-164
Smith, B.; wife	26 Aug. 1897	H-618
Smith, Mrs. Barbary, married	31 May 1875	C-405
Smith, Mrs. Bertha; Francis G.	10 Jan. 1901	I-312
Smith, Bertha E., administrix, est. of Wm. J.	22 Mar. 1904	J-7
Smith, Climena; J. B. (D-50)	12 Feb. 1876	C-492
Smith, Colman D., widower	24 Apr. 1861	A-341
Smith, D. I., married	25 Mar. 1870	B-388
Smith, W. J.; Deliah T. (E-518)	16 Jan. 1884	E-423
Smith, E. I., married	17 Feb. 1874	C-287
Smith, Eleanor Isabel; Roland H.	10 Aug. 1914	L-95
Smith, Ellen; Thomas J.	8 Nov. 1875	C-453
Smith, Emma M.; W. H.	17 Aug. 1878	D-307

Applicant and Family Information	Filing Date	Vol.-Pg.
Smith, Emmett C., unmarried	6 Sep. 1906	J-151
Smith. Eugene W.; wife	1 June 1888	F-473
Smith, F. W.; Mary	6 Feb. 1880	D-516
Smith, Florence L., husband Temple	20 Feb. 1917	L-334
Smith, Frank L., widower; 2 children	11 Dec. 1908	K-193
Smith, Hazel E.; Wm. J.; Hazel M. 7, Henry 6, Helen 5	25 Oct. 1915	L-222
Smith, Henry J., married	21 June 1871	B-543
Smith, Irwin C.; Christine (D-115)	9 Dec. 1871	B-570
Smith, James M.; wife	27 Oct. 1879	D-481
Smith, Jessie L.; J. H.	29 July 1918	L-419
Smith, Mrs. J. E.; W. N.	19 June 1894	H-61
Smith, John F.; wife	4 Mar. 1884	E-445
Smith, John T.; Emeline	19 Jan. 1877	D-76
Smith, Joseph Gay, married	7 Aug. 1871	B-553
Smith, Margaret; Peter	19 June 1884	F-11
Smith, Mary; T. W.	20 Feb. 1880	D-528
Smith, Mary A.; widow of Robert E.	2 Apr. 1864	A-599
Smith, Mary Ann; W. N.	30 Mar. 1876	C-507
Smith, Mary C.; Michael G.	13 Apr. 1914	L-74
Smith, Mary E.; John K.	6 Sep. 1918	L-428
Smith, Mary E.; Thomas (E-127; E-73)	3 July 1873	C-184
Smith, Mary Frances; John M.	19 Sep. 1917	L-370
Smith, Mary W.; insolvent debtor (H-126); probate	14 Feb. 1895	F-227
Smith, Mrs. Nellie; Arthur E.	12 July 1900	I-729
Smith, Nellie M.; R. Press	1 Mar. 1895	H-279
Smith, N. O.; wife	16 Mar. 1885	F-40
Smith, Pauline J.; Geo. N.	17 Aug. 1901	I-350
Smith, Ralph; Catharine	27 Mar. 1873	C-131
Smith; Rebecca; Wm. A.	2 Sep. 1875	C-436
Smith, S. J. (I); Margaret Ann	26 Jan. 1861	A-112
Smith, Samuel J.	3 Mar. 1866	A-697
Smith, Samuel II; wife	3 Jan. 1888	F-441
Smith, Sarah C.; C. J.	4 Nov. 1905	J-103
Smith, Stephen; Mary (A-415; B-502)	1 Nov. 1860	A-45
Smith, Teresa M.; J. K.	29 July 1882	E-250
Smith, Thomas S.; Delia	31 Oct. 1917	L-378
Smith, Thos. W.; Mary	27 May 1861	A-367
Smith, W. A. C.; Orpa A.	31 Jan. 1866	A-692
Smith, W. E.; Mae	6 July 1916	L-291

Applicant and Family Information	Filing Date	Vol.-Pg.
Smith, William J., married	22 July 1862	A-498
Smith, Wm; wife	29 Aug. 1898	I-114
Smith, Wm. R.; Minerva	12 Nov. 1867	B-167
Smithers, Ellen D.; Geo. E.	28 May 1886	F-263
Smyth, Charles S., married	2 May 1878	B-672
Smyth, Louise L.; Oscar A.	16 June 1913	L-9
Snider, Adaline, unmarried; head of family	14 Sep. 1900	I-291
Snook, Margaret; W. P.	24 May 1877	D-131
Snyder, Bessie M.; Herbert B.	25 Oct. 1918	L-444
Snyder, Rosy F., widow; 4 minors	16 Jan. 1912	K-410
Soderman, Marie Christine; F. A.	24 Aug. 1911	K-387
Soernsen, Fred Wm.; Alma K.	15 Feb. 1915	L-145
Sohlke, Theredore; husband D. H.	25 Mar. 1861	A-174
Soldati, Luigia; Alexander; probate	7 Mar. 1904	H-243
Solomon, Charles; Emma L.	28 June 1907	K-56
Soloman, Mrs. Sarah A.; Charles	30 Jan. 1899	I-171
Somerville, Robert; Mary Jane; children: Jennie Coleman, James Robert, Wm. S.	16 Sep. 1912	K-449
Somes, Geo. R.; no mention of family	12 Nov. 1897	I-16
Somoza, V, Maria de; hus. Fernando (note: Maria de is wife)	11 Oct. 1918	L-435
Soracco, F. W.; Katie H.; 1 child: Clarence T., age 14	30 Dec. 1909	K-285
Soules, Albert; wife	23 Dec. 1884	E-533
Southard, Josephine L.; J. B.	7 Jan. 1861	A-98
Southern, Anne A., Thomas R.	3 June 1895	H-225
Souza, Etelvina; M. C.	20 Aug. 1895	H-264
Sowash, Rosa E.; Frank	24 Feb. 1915	L-146
Sparks, Mary A.; John W.	13 May 1905	J-70
Sparks, Sarah J.; husband F. M.; minor child	28 Dec. 1917	L-389
Spaulding, Maude Trice; Lewis W.	10 May 1920	M-31
Spence, Andy T.; wife	28 June 1890	G-62
Spencer, Benjamin, married	2 Nov. 1872	C-125
Spencer, E. A.; husband J. L.	7 Jan. 1919	L-453
Spencer, Jennie; Henry	30 Dec. 1912	K-479
Spencer, Julia E.; Robt. A.	1 Nov. 1915	L-223
Spencer, Mary C.; married	25 Oct. 1871	C-14
Spencer, Otis, married	16 Feb. 1871	B-496
Spencer, Nellie M.; Byron M. (H-329)	6 Aug. 1877	C-581
Spickerman, Harvey; wife	4 Apr. 1879	D-393
Spillane, Belle; John	8 July 1889	F-604

Applicant and Family Information	Filing Date	Vol.-Pg.
Spiller, Frank F.; wife	18 Apr. 1882	E-208
Spotswood, A.; wife	19 Sep. 1888	F-509
Spotswood, Mary; Robert	30 July 1878	D-301
Spotswood, Robert, married (C-118; C-331)	1 Jan. 1872	C-24
Spottswood, Mary E.; Thomas Hopper	19 Oct. 1897	I-3
Sprague, Edith B.; Edwin E.; 2 children .(6/10/1907, K-50)	21 May 1900	I-273
Sprauer, L. R.; Cordelia	7 Oct. 1913	L-36
Spring, Ada May; Elias Wheelock Spring	10 Oct. 1905	J-101
Spring, Mrs. Fannie E.; head of family; 1 minor son (J-81)	8 Mar. 1900	I-252
Springer, Frank; Hilaria C.; 2 children: Christoph M. 13, Caroline B. 10	17 Dec. 1913	L-49
Springer, James L., married	7 Sep. 1872	B-603
Sproule, Joseph Alexander; Jane Earl, wife	19 Apr. 1861	A-247
Spurr, Wm. P.; Sarah E.	19 Apr. 1862	A-449
Squires, Ella; E. C.	23 Oct. 1884	E-516
Squires, Ella; 2 children; no husband	23 Dec. 1897	I-29
Sroufe, David W.; Adelia A. (11/18/1872, B-607)	4 Mar. 1867	B-90
Staedler, Elizabeth; John G.	23 July 1874	D-657
Staendli, Richard H.; wife	9 May 1896	H-411
Staley, Winnie M.; Charles E.	27 Mar. 1907	K-37
Standard, Jennie M.; J. D.	13 July 1914	L-92
Stanley, Josiah, married	16 Nov. 1868	B-278
Stanley, Mrs. Lucy J., widow of J. N.	14 Jan. 1886	F-201
Stanley, William B., married	21 Jan. 1876	C-482
Stapleton, Johanna; Patrick	21 Apr. 1877	D-109
Stapp, Martha A.; husband	30 Sep. 1878	D-335
Starke, Francis; August	31 Dec. 1866	B-56
Starke, Frederick; Mena	4 Feb. 1861	A-117
Starkie, Frances; Auguste	25 Mar. 1861	A-172
Starr, Theodore C.; Mary E. (Theodore, dec'd 7/23/1890, D592, probate); 4 children	19 Oct. 1888	F-511
Stearns, F. R.; Ida A.	13 Nov. 1896	H-503
Steele, Julius; Elizabeth	22 Dec. 1875	C-470
Steffan, Rossa; mother and sister	17 Apr. 1903	I-448
Steiger, Edward, married	19 Feb. 1874	C-283
Steinbring, William; Amelia	30 Mar. 1904	J-9
Steinweg, Ernest/Ernst; Wilhelmine; daughter Helene L., 3 years; Frida J., 4 months	18 Aug. 1913	L-23
Sterling, P. W., married (P. W. dec'd 6/11/1888, D-422 P probate; 10/29/1879 D-473)	24 Aug. 1867	B-156

Applicant and Family Information	Filing Date	Vol.-Pg.
Stevens, Charles L., head of family; minor child	22 July 1885	F-99
Stevens, Frances, widow	8 Sep. 1915	L-212
Stevens, Henry D., married	15 Jan. 1862	A-394
Stevenson, Joseph O., married	25 June 1872	C-109
Stevenson, Guy; May	15 July 1918	L-414
Stewart, C; wife	13 July 1882	E-242
Stewart, Ethel; Charles F.; two minor	19 Oct. 1912	K-464
Stewart, Hannah N., married	28 Mar. 1874	C-300
Stewart, Julia, widow	28 Sep. 1880	E-38
Stewart, Sarah; John	15 Nov. 1870	D-463
Stewart, William; wife	28 Nov. 1881	E-162
Stickney, A. O., married	13 Feb. 1867	B-88
Stier, Anna H.; Gottolb/Gottlob	1 Apr. 1885	F-43
Stiles, R. P.; Mrs. Fannie	14 Mar. 1887	F-370
Stillwell, Annie; V.	13 Feb. 1880	D-523
Stockdale, Hugh (dec'd); Carrie; executor Sherman G. Stockdale; (7/18/1891, E-184 probate)	17 June 1873	C-171
Stocker, Belle A.; husband James T.	30 Oct. 1908	K-180
Stocking, George; Mary E.	18 July 1918	L-417
Stoddard, Louisa J., married	5 July 1877	C-565
Stofen, John J.; Alice	26 Sep. 1877	D-153
Stafford, N. O.; Mary Ann	16 Apr. 1861	A-219
Stoffregen, J. F.; Jennie D. F.; Alice F., 10 years	8 Nov. 1920	M-57
Stolker, Ernestine; William, dec'd; no minors; probate	15 Nov. 1897	G-42
Stombs, E. H., married	1 Aug. 1865	A-666
Stone, Hannah E.; J. F.	21 July 1920	M-44
Stone, J. M.; wife	11 Apr. 1902	I-383
Stone, Nathan J.; wife	14 Oct. 1881	E-152
Stone, Rosie A.; Willard P.	28 May 1903	I-454
Stone, M. D.; Sarah J.	7 Dec. 1881	E-155
Stoneberg, Carl Ferdinand Theodore; Anna	4 Apr. 1905	J-58
Storch, Johanna N.; Hugo W. (L-306)	13 Oct. 1915	L-221
Story, Catherine; Stephen C.	12 June 1908	K-131
Story, Susan B., married	27 July 1868	B-252
Stover, Charles; Julia	9 Feb. 1863	A-539
Stowell, George H., head of family	26 Oct. 1869	B-358
Strading, Anna; W. C.; four minors (K-491)	29 Apr. 1907	K-41
Stratton, Mrs. Nellie; F. W.	15 Jan. 1894	H-18
Stratton, William A., married	25 Sep. 1868	B-267

Applicant and Family Information	Filing Date	Vol.-Pg.
Strege, Bertha; August	18 Jan. 1918	L-393
Streeter, George, head of family; three sons, three daughters	28 Mar. 1916	L-266
Stridde, Charles; wife	5 Jan. 1880	D-503
Strider, Anna M.; George A.	20 Oct. 1900	I-299
Striening, John N.; Caroline E.	5 Sep. 1900	I-290
Strohl, George Washington; Laura	26 May 1909	K-230
Stromgren, Jennie; Gust	3 Dec. 1895	H-325
Stromgren, C. J., Jr.; M. Christa	3 Dec. 1895	H-327
Stuart, Absalom B.; Anabel McGaughy, wife (10/24/1887, D-368, probate)	28 Apr. 1883	E-329
Stuart, James F.; Sarah	20 Feb. 1861	A-132
Stump, Conrad, married	5 Apr. 1866	B-8
Stump, Henry, married	22 Jan. 1866	B-80
Stump, James; Christiana	24 June 1869	B-337
Studdart, Michael; married	10 Sep. 1878	D-322
Studdert, J. T.; wife; two children	15 Sep. 1911	K-391
Studdert, Mary E.; Burt	11 Dec. 1883	E-406
Studebaker, Margaret F.; John	24 Feb. 1913	K-488
Stump, Charles E.; Cora E.; minor children, Charles A., Genevieve	29 Apr. 1912	K-423
Stump, Bridget, married (re-recorded from Book C-423)	6 June 1875	D-20
Stump, Flora B.; Leonard P.	8 Aug. 1888	F-484
Stump, John A.; Minnie S. Haub	2 May 1901	I-325
Stump, Samuel W.; Susan C.	7 Feb. 1891	G-166
Sturgeon, Henry; Annie B.	6 Sep. 1880	E-35
Sturman, Benjamin; family	22 Dec. 1876	D-64
Stylsvig, Christ Wm.; Ellen Marie	27 Apr. 1896	H-404
Suers, Manuel; wife	3 Jan. 1898	I-37
Sullivan, Frank A.; Mary E.; Mary, Frances, Harvey, Pauline, Edward	26 Apr. 1909	K-226
Sullivan, Kate, head of family; minor children	10 Sep. 1890	G-112
Sullivan, Mary (wife of John?)	11 Oct. 1886	F-314
Sullivan, P. J.; wife	9 June 1885	F-73
Sullivan, Patrick; Ellen	15 Sep.1877	D-146
Summerfield, Elva; E. J.	13 Mar. 1911	K-371
Sund, Edna O.; Alfred D.	29 Sep. 1909	K-265
Sundborg, Chas.; wife	19 Sep. 1891	G-230
Sunde, T. Evenson; Esther Marie	20 Apr. 1917	L-263
Surryhne, Eliz. Melina; Edward dec'd; minor children: Hiram,	29 Sep. 1898	G-223

Applicant and Family Information	Filing Date	Vol.-Pg.
Mary, John; probate		
Sutherland, J. J.; wife	20 Nov. 1893	H-8
Sutherland, Mary C.; John J.	25 Oct. 1887	F-423
Sutherland, Mary T., widow	4 Oct. 1912	K-457
Sutherland, Myrtie L.; Robt. G. (12/31/1910, abandonment)	29 Jan. 1896	H-375
Sutherland, W. H.; Ellen; probate	7 May 1885	D-119
Sutton, May; H. A.	6 July 1901	I-339
Swain, Aaron; Mary A.	4 Apr. 1872	C-68
Swain, R. M.; wife	21 Feb. 1890	G-11
Swain, Wm. C.; Sarah	26 Apr. 1861	A-333
Swan, W. G., married	20 Mar. 1878	D-239
Swanson, Ella; Carl O.	4 Oct. 1906	K-3
Swanson, Gertrude I.; Andrew J.; children: Gertrude, Robert, Clarine, George	24 Feb. 1914	L-62
Swaysgood, Susanna; John W.; adult child.; Myrtle E., minor age 16; probate	24 Mar. 1896	F-403
Sweeney, T. F.; Grace C.	24 Feb. 1921	M-76
Sweeney, Tessie; Edward S.	27 Dec. 1906	K-27
Sweet, Manly A.; Mary Ann	20 Aug. 1860	A-19
Sweetman, C. H., married	3 Aug. 1863	A-559
Sweetser, E. D.; wife	21 Dec. 1903	I-487
Swett, Fannie J.; Ebin (F-114-Div., head of family, 3 minors)	15 July 1881	E-114
Swett, Frank H.; wife	3 Feb. 1882	E-186
Swift, Frederick; wife	11 Apr. 1905	J-62
Switzer, John; Eliza	6 July 1906	J-140

Applicant and Family Information	Filing Date	Vol.-Pg.
Tabacchi, Domenico; Rachael/Rachele; 2 minors (L-401)	11 Oct. 1916	L-308
Taber, John S.; Isabella (D-479, probate)	25 May 1876	C-524
Taggart, John, married	3 Oct. 1871	B-566
Talbot, Mary W.; Kennedy B.	6 Nov. 1872	D-10
Tarbett, F. B. (P.); wife	14 June 1879	D-426
Tarrant, H. F.; married	5 July 1877	C-572
Tarzyn, Joseph; Anna	27 May 1913	L-1
Tatum, Miriam T.; husband F. P.	15 Nov. 1915	L-231
Taylor, Lewis K.; Catharine O'Brien Taylor	11 Apr. 1866	A-699
Taylor, Chas. H.; Elsano	16 Oct. 1860	A-40
Taylor, Frances A.; John	30 May 1878	D-262
Taylor, Gertie C.; John D.	26 May 1913	K-506
Taylor, Luther, married	1 Dec. 1862	A-521
Taylor, Martha M.; Daniel S.	3 Aug. 1883	E-359
Taylor, Nannie C.; John S.	17 Nov. 1900	I-305
Taylor, S. F.; Ruth S.; 3 minors	6 Apr. 1917	L-342
Taylor, W. H. H.; Maria	8 Aug. 1887	F-403
Teague, C. P.; wife	15 Oct. 1879	D-474
Teale, Kate L.; G. W.	19 Feb. 1898	I-54
Tellefson, Oscar T.; Julia; 1 child	2 Feb. 1915	L-140
Tempel, Conrad; wife	1 Apr. 1895	H-203
Tennant, Richard Edward; wife	5 June 1882	E-226
Tennant, Rosa A.; Wm.	15 May 1901	I-329
Tenney, John M.; wife	20 Nov. 1902	I-423
Terry, J. W.; wife	21 Mar. 1879	D-390
Terry, John L.; America	1 Sep. 1865	A-675
Tharp, Sarah F.; Scott M.	23 Jan. 1909	K-198
Thatcher, David; C. A., wife	19 Mar. 1872	C-61
Thayer, F. L., unmarried (H-115)	29 June 1885	F-86
Thayer, Franklin L.; Elizabeth A.	2 Feb. 1872	C-39
Thielemann, Henrietta; Christian	5 Apr. 1861	A-204
Thierkoff, Frank G.; M. A., wife	1 Mar. 1871	B-505
Thiessen, Friedrich; wife	10 Feb. 1899	I-179
Thilo, Anna; C. A. (notarization: C. J.)	25 Mar. 1901	I-320
Thing, Sarah J., married (see F-130; E-164)	9 Mar. 1878	D-229
Thistle, James M.; Mary	20 Aug. 1878	B-345
Thom, Charles J.; Elizabeth B.	3 Feb. 1910	K-293
Thomas, Alfred R.; Pearl; 2 children	3 Jan. 1916	L-323

Applicant and Family Information	Filing Date	Vol.-Pg.
Thomas, Alonzo; A. M. (B-544)	10 Feb. 1865	A-638
Thomas, Carolina; Joseph (Carolina E. aka Caroline)	1 May 1893	G-414
Thomas, J. S.; wife	5 Dec. 1903	I-485
Thomas, Triennial T.; Herbert O.	23 Dec. 1915	L-246
Thomas, Warren S.; Mary Jane (C-105)	14 Sep. 1861	A-379
Thompson, Thomas L.; wife	5 June 1879	D-422
Thompson, A. W., married	1 June 1866	B-16
Thompson, Albert; Annie (K-381)	9 Mar. 1911	K-367
Thompson, Abram W., married	8 Feb. 1878	D-218
Thompson, Annie; Albert	15 Jan. 1912	K-409
Thompson, Annie; Albert	20 Jan. 1913	K-483
Thompson, Edgar I.; Caroline	19 June 1914	L-86
Thompson, Edward; Kate E.	26 Feb. 1900	I-247
Thompson, Eliza; I. H.	12 Nov. 1869	B-365
Thompson, Frank; Juanita	22 Jan. 1915	L-136
Thompson, G. W., married	27 Oct. 1876	D-49
Thompson, J. C.; wife	12 Nov. 1897	I-13
Thompson, J. H.; Eliza	3 Dec. 1866	B-73
Thompson, James D.; Mary Elalina (1/2/1874, C-239)	14 Mar. 1861	A-158
Thompson, M. J.; J. S.	25 June 1888	F-474
Thompson, Martha; E. G. C.	25 July 1883	E-357
Thompson, Mary Jane; J. S.	27 Aug. 1880	E-31
Thompson, Matilda E.; Jefferson A., dec'd, probate	13 June 1898	G-179
Thompson, N. M.; Charles	3 July 1905	J-82
Thompson, Nellie B.; John S. C.	8 Nov. 1909	K-275
Thompson, R.; wife	17 Apr. 1882	E-207
Thompson, Robt. A.; wife	14 Aug. 1884	E-495
Thompson, Thos B.; Elizabeth	17 Apr. 1861	A-241
Thompson, Thomas L.; wife	5 June 1879	D-422
Thonley, Henry; Mary	12 Apr. 1861	A-224
Thomson, Mary A.; Jens (K-33)	11 May 1898	I-71
Thomson, Edwin P.; Mary	9 Feb. 1887	F-355
Thorman, J. H. C.; Anna	17 June 1912	K-429
Thorne, Mary A.; C. L.	10 Nov. 1888	F-519
Thornley, Mary, widow of Henry	28 Apr. 1862	A-481
Thorpe, Caroline A. M. P.; William (D-450)	1 May 1878	B-671
Thrift, Sabin D.; wife	22 May 1882	E-220
Thurston, Amelia S.; Andrew; probate	25 Nov. 1893	F-21

Thurston, Edna; Geo. B.	31 Mar. 1894	H-42
Tibbits, Mrs. Ollie; Charles A.	4 Jan. 1918	L-390
Tickner, Daniel, married	15 Jan. 1872	B-585
Tidball, Lois E.; Chas. B.	29 Feb. 1904	J-5
Tighe, Kelley, married	6 Nov. 1866	B-51
Tighe, Annie; Kelly	3 Feb. 1890	G-5
Tocchini, Assunta; A. H. aka Arideo	25 Sep. 1918	L-430
Todd, Alice Fiske; husband	18 July 1899	I-211
Todd, James M.; Mary J.	16 Dec. 1915	L-243
Tomblinson, Rena L.; husband	13 Aug. 1894	H-87
Tomblison, Samuel; wife (G-49, probate)	14 May 1886	F-261
Toombs, Sarah J.; H. C.	24 Apr. 1891	G-185
Torliatt, Adrienne; Peter (K-354)	9 June 1904	J-19
Toroni, Margherita; Bartolomejo	28 Oct. 1898	G-474
Torrance, Mrs. J. L.; Joseph L.	26 Nov. 1914	I-153
Tourady, Ida M.; J. M.	12 Nov. 1914	L-114
Tovani, Ella; Romvaldo (I-389)	7 Apr. 1887	F-386
Towne, Smith D.; Amanda H. Towne	22 Apr. 1861	A-344
Towne, Smith D., married	15 July 1870	B-429
Tracy, Wm. N., married	21 Aug. 1879	D-454
Trambley, Thomas, married	26 Nov. 1875	C-460
Traser, Philipp; wife	7 Dec. 1899	I-229
Trautner, Max; Frances	18 Oct. 1911	K-394
Travis, Anne, widow	24 Sep. 1878	D-331
Treadway, Griffin; Elizabeth	16 Apr. 1861	A-228
Treadway, Nancy J.; Richard M.	21 Dec. 1861	A-390
Treadway, Sarah; Daniel G.	4 Jan. 1898	I-41
Treibig, Susan K.; Lorenzo G.	19 June 1884	F-10
Treub, Henry; Susana	23 Apr. 1877	B-117
Trevor, Frank; Mary A.	14 Mar. 1860	A-154
Trine, Eula E.; Oliver P.	27 Dec. 1915	L-247
Trinque/Tringue, Margaret; W. D., husband	27 Jan. 1862	A-396
Trotter, Sarah E.; Richard	21 July 1890	F-631
Trowbridge, Emma B.; George T.	8 Apr. 1916	L-264
Trowbridge, Geo. Otis; Louisa Maria (E-429)	18 May 1883	E-336
Trowbridge, Geo. T.; wife	31 Jan. 1884	E-428
Truell, Geo., insolvent debtor	23 Dec. 1886	F-346
Truell, Laura; Geo. R.	14 Jan. 1886	F-203
Truett, Mortimer K., married	26 Jan. 1869	B-310

Truitt, James H., married	27 Aug. 1866	B-42
Truitt, Mary E.; Eugene R.	9 Nov. 1905	J-107
Truitt, Miers F.; Salena G.	22 Jan. 1863	A-529
Truitt, Roland K.; Sinai; 3 minors (F-590, L-497)	21 June 1875	C-410
Tucker, Harold G.; Mattie W.	6 Nov. 1919	M-10
Tucker, Henry T.; wife	2 Apr. 1892	G-309
Tupper, G. A., married (F-534)	2 Dec. 1875	C-441
Turman, Benjamin C., married	22 Dec. 1866	B-52
Turnbull, Susan; Thomas	31 Aug. 1891	G-224
Turner, C. F.; Libbie M.	31 Oct. 1913	L-39
Turner, C. F.; Libbie M.	10 Nov. 1905	J-108
Turner, C. F.; Libbie M.	12 Aug. 1918	L-425
Turner, C. F.; Libbie M.	9 Aug. 1904	J-25
Turner, J. M.; wife	22 Apr. 1897	H-577
Turner, John; Harriet C. (see C-235)	7 Sep. 1874	C-327
Turner, Peter W.; married	8 May 1876	B-664
Tustin, Isaac; Josephine	18 Dec. 1862	A-525
Turner, John, married; elderly sister	2 Mar. 1894	H-30
Turner, Robert Wilson; Ada Maude	16 Sep. 1920	M-50
Turner, Samantha E., head of family	19 Apr. 1888	F-464
Turner, W. J.; Susan E.	7 Jan. 1893	G-391
Tuttle, Florence McLeod; Lauren T., husband	16 Apr. 1915	L-164
Tuttle, Permilia A.; Jeremiah	17 Mar. 1890	G-26
Tuomey, Catherine; Bertholoma, husband	24 Mar. 1880	D-542
Tuller, Jas. M.; Alisha	15 July 1861	A-373
Tuller, James M.; 2 minors of whom he is father	23 Nov. 1863	A-572
Tustin, Columbus	10 Jan. 1864	A-585
Tyler, Flora E.; Joseph Leander	17 Feb. 1904	J-1
Tyther, Joseph; Honora	15 Nov. 1884	E-521

Applicant and Family Information	Filing Date	Vol.-Pg.
Uhl, Felix, married	3 May 1876	B-663
Ulberg, Henry O.; wife	15 Mar. 1895	H-201
Ullrich, Geo.; Elizabeth (Geo. 12/6/1895, F-356, probate,; 6/27/1895, H-237)	20 Dec. 1893	G-486
Ulrich, Jacob; Hannah	2 Apr. 1872	C-65
Ungewitter, Mary; H. W.	21 Oct. 1890	G-135
Unwiller, Lavinia, widow of Wm. M.; 1 dau. Edna May	20 July 1908	K-146
Upson, Julia; Chas.	16 Jan. 1911	K-361
Upson, Madeg P.; Chas.	9 Nov. 1895	H-316
Ure, S. A.; Chas. S.		I-281
Urton, Sarah L.; John H.	24 July 1900	K-442
Urton, William L., married	29 Apr. 1876	B-661
Ury, Mary E.; J. G.	25 Mar. 1893	G-406

Applicant and Family Information	Filing Date	Vol.-Pg.
Vail, Anna B.; Albert H. (D-595, probate)	17 Feb. 1875	C-372
Valdes, Mercedes D., widow; 4 children (not named)	30 Nov. 1901	I-365
Valenti, Emma; Domenico	9 May 1903	I-451
Valentine, Mary G., widow	15 Sep. 1880	E-37
Valkos, Sophie, head of family; 1 minor son	18 June 1920	M-41
Valley, Rachel, unmarried	25 Mar. 1880	D-544
Vallier, Mary Ann, widow of Alexander	15 May 1899	I-205
Van Allen, John J.; wife	6 Dec. 1862	A-522
Van Allen, Wm., head of family, has care of father John J.	28 Mar. 1892	G-304
Van Bebber/Bibber, Peter; Esmeralda	6 Sep. 1887	F-413
Van Buren, Jessie H.; Edwin G.	28 Aug. 1908	K-159
Van de Mark, Geo. F.; wife	21 Oct. 1899	I-221
Van der Hoof, Martin V.; Azella M.	18 Nov. 1899	I-226
Van Doren, Frances M.; John S.	23 Aug. 1886	F-299
Van Eps, John S.; wife	4 Feb. 1895	H-163
Van Every, A. J.; wife	29 Aug. 1881	E-132
Van Mater, John, married	17 Apr. 1868	B-225
Van Marter, Josie L.; Wm. H.	29 Feb. 1892	G-300
Van Valkenburgh, Hester; Noah, husband; all children over 27 yrs.; probate	24 Feb. 1896	F-387
Van Voast, Elle; Wm.	5 Feb. 1884	E-433
Van Winkle, Thos.; Polly Ann, wife	20 Apr. 1861	A-279
Vanderhoof, Azella M.; Martin V.	18 Nov. 1899	I-226
Vanderkarr, James; Grace S.	5 Sep. 1912	K-446
Vanderleith, Elese; John	20 Mar. 1905	J-57
Vanoni, Mary; Thomas	26 Jan. 1900	I-236
Vasilatos, Louise; N.	16 Nov. 1909	K-277
Varner, Margaret; Samuel	24 Nov. 1891	G-272
Vasques, Catharine; Pedro J.	6 Aug. 1860	A-14
Vasser, J. R.; Charlotte J.	20 Dec. 1888	F-525
Vaughn, Louisa F.; J. H.	20 Feb. 1876	D-85
Vaughn, Martha Ann Adeline; Daniel	2 Apr. 1869	B-322
Veatch, Geo. W.; Clarrisa	19 Feb. 1861	A-122
Venezia, Mary; Giavonni, aka John; his child Rose, age 9 (K-502)	17 Sep. 1913	L-30
Ventura, Mrs. Mamie; Joseph	2 Jan. 1907	K-90
Vesper, Blanche; David W.	12 Nov. 1919	M-11
Vincent, Anna D., widow, possibly of Jose (deed from Jose mentioned)	3 May 1910	K-318

Applicant and Family Information	Filing Date	Vol.-Pg.
Viola, Marietta; Salvadori	5 May 1900	I-272
Violetti, Angiolina; G.	29 Dec. 1897	I-35
Voight, Lena	19 Mar. 1897	H-559
Volk, Lisette K.; W. J.	5 Nov. 1892	G-368
Von Grafen, Mrs. Anna B.; Wm. Henry	14 Mar. 1903	I-436
Von Hacht, Heinrich; wife	11 Apr. 1902	I-384
Von Ottenfeld, Katie, unmarried	8 Sep. 1919	L-494
Von Tillow, Lillian E.; W. W.	2 Aug. 1909	K-246
Vragnison, Girol A.; wife	28 Nov. 1883	E-403

Applicant and Family Information	Filing Date	Vol.-Pg.
Waddell, Alexander J., married (F-120)	11 Oct. 1877	D-162
Waddell, John Hope; wife (F-354)	3 Oct. 1881	E-145
Wade, Wm.; Louise	25 Feb. 1908	K-101
Wagenseller, Clara S., married	23 Feb. 1872	C-49
Wagers, Derral D.; Amy A.	28 Feb. 1908	K-103
Wagers, O. G.; wife	1 Nov. 1904	J-42
Waggle, Wm. M., married	18 Feb. 1862	A-403
Wagner, Ida; Theodore	16 Oct. 1900	I-292
Wait, Leavitt, unmarried	18 Nov. 1861	A-385
Wakeland, Sadie R.; John J.	24 June 1907	K-54
Wakeland, Sarah P., widow	24 Aug. 1909	K-250
Walden, Abbie E.; F. J.	25 Feb. 1903	I-431
Walker, Alonzo; Elizabeth	3 Apr. 1861	A-186
Walker, Anna J.; W. A.	26 Jan. 1912	K-411
Walker, Chas. A., married	18 Aug. 1873	C-204
Walker, E. S.; wife	2 Feb. 1882	E-185
Walker, L. F.; Sarah F.	9 Oct. 1901	I-358
Walker, Lucinda; E. S., husband, probate	25 Feb. 1897	F-521
Walker, Lydia J.; L. W.	21 Nov. 1888	F-569
Walker, Mary Frances; Edward L.	26 May 1897	H-595
Walker, Mary M.; Oscar	5 Sep. 1882	E-259
Walker, Olive Ingram; W. Y.	21 June 1905	J-78
Wall, E. T., married	4 Oct. 1878	D-340
Wallace, Cynthia D.; J. F.	21 Apr. 1909	K-223
Wallace, Homer; Jessie	2 Aug. 1920	M-47
Wallace, W. Wm.; Louisa I.	26 Apr. 1862	A-476
Wallace, Wm., married	14 July 1877	C-573
Walldorf, Philipp; wife	7 May 1880	D-566
Walker, Richard C.; Myrtle Ensign Walker	15 June 1914	L-85
Walsh, Catherine, widow; husband, Michael dec'd, probate; children: Katie, John, Patrick, Julia and Nellie	9 Jan. 1899	G-262
Walsh, Michael; Mary	20 May 1876	C-519
Walsh, M., insolvent debtor	19 Nov. 1889	F-627
Walsh, M. (male); family of 6 children	18 Dec. 1897	I-28
Waltenspiel, Alexander A.; family of 3 children	19 June 1902	I-406
Walton, J. F., head of household; minor child: James, Everett, Conger	26 Apr. 1910	K-314
Waltzer, Emil; Elizabeth; no children	30 June 1915	L-188
Wands, James, married	5 Aug. 1870	B-437

Applicant and Family Information	Filing Date	Vol.-Pg.
Ward, C. W.; Rebecca	24 July 1872	C-114
Ward, Charles, married	2 Feb. 1878	D-214
Ward, Mrs. Eva; W. H.	6 Jan. 1896	H-343
Ward, Ira T.; wife	10 Jan. 1888	F-444
Ward, John; Susan	3 Jan. 1880	D-501
Ward, Lelah B.; Arthur E.	17 Dec. 1915	L-245
Ward, Luther L.; wife	26 Jan. 1888	F-452
Ward, Rachel; H. T.	10 Jan. 1877	D-72
Ward, Thomas; wife	14 July 1880	E-22
Warden, William Dexter; wife	8 Dec. 1880	E-51
Ware, A. B.; wife	23 Jan. 1879	D-378
Ware, Catherine F.; Wm.	7 Mar. 1885	F-30
Warfield, Luta E. E.; R. E., husband	7 Aug. 1883	E-362
Warnekros, N.; A., wife	20 Dec. 1876	D-92
Warner, Mrs. Annie; Joseph L.	17 Feb. 1897	H-544
Warner, Gustavus, married	31 Jan. 1867	B-81
Warren, John B., married	15 May 1871	B-522
Warren, Mary Ann, single	7 Nov. 1893	G-478
Warren, C. D.; Susan B.	15 Mar. 1867	B-94
Warren, George F.; Maude Ryall	27 Nov. 1908	K-187
Warren, Thomas H.; Minnie	4 Dec. 1911	K-404
Washer, Bridget, married	24 Aug. 1872	B-593
Washer, Bridget; Horatio	20 June 1873	C-175
Washer, Catherine; Henry	22 Apr. 1862	A-461
Washer, Henry; Mrs. Dora D.	22 Jan. 1879	D-376
Waters, Catharine, a widow	19 Mar. 1861	A-171
Watkins, J. O.; wife	7 Apr. 1897	H-564
Watson, Mrs. Clara I.; W. A., husband	4 Apr. 1918	L-405
Watson, Greenville; wife	2 Oct. 1882	E-269
Watson, James Reade, head of family; mother	3 Jan. 1895	H-132
Watson, James S.; Lucinday F.	24 Jan. 1885	E-545
Watson, Mary; L. J.	27 June 1905	J-79
Watson, Rhoda A.; J. A.	6 Aug. 1897	H-600
Wattles, Benjamin C.; Mary S.	19 Mar. 1862	A-408
Watts, Benjamin Franklin, married	3 Jan. 1868	B-178
Waugh, Lorenzo; Clarissa	11 Sep. 1877	D-151
Weaver, Louisa, not married; sister Alice Weaver	25 Sep. 1914	L-106
Webb, Arabel; H. J.	28 Oct. 1902	I-418

Applicant and Family Information	Filing Date	Vol.-Pg.
Webb, Mary O.; Wm. R.	19 Jan. 1886	F-206
Webb, Rachel R.; husband	13 Nov. 1884	E-519
Weber, Sophie; Henry	11 Sep. 1906	J-152
Wedge, Anna; John J.	27 June 1918	L-411
Wedehase, F.; wife	30 Mar. 1903	I-439
Weeks, Cynthia B.; S. S.	12 Oct. 1891	G-242
Weeks, Lewis; wife	21 Jan. 1897	H-522
Weeks, S. S., married	23 Oct. 1876	D-46
Weeks, Wm. C., married	28 June 1870	B-427
Wehrspon, August; Agnes, wife	1 June 1914	L-82
Weigand, Mary; Charles	8 July 1878	D-288
Weir, Mary; James	31 Jan. 1868	B-191
Weise, Lisette; Christian; minor Lisette; probate	28 May 1894	F-128
Welch, Mary; Richard	30 Aug. 1869	B-346
Weller, Sarah M.; Silas	19 Oct. 1875	C-448
Welling, John, married	5 Oct. 1867	B-141
Wells, Catherine Eliz; Clark	9 Sep. 1879	D-462
Wells, Mrs. Nancy V., widow; granddaughter Hazel F.Wells	8 Nov. 1915	L-226
Wells, Olive; Stilson	23 July 1878	D-298
Wells, Stilson; wife (J-113)	7 May 1895	H-218
Wells, Wm R.; Ruzella C.	30 Nov. 1860	A-67
Welsholt, Margaret; Theodore	18 Aug. 1860	A-18
Weltz, Rosina; Geo (K-355)	24 July 1903	I-457
Wentworth, F. G., married	3 Mar. 1870	B-382
Wenzel, Julius; wife	2 Oct. 1894	G-504
Werner, Frank, reside with mother/sister	17 Apr. 1903	I-448
Wescoatt, Margery Ann; Jonas	7 Nov. 1892	G-371
Wescott, Oliver; wife	25 Jan. 1881	E-67
West, Augusta Werner; William Walter	9 Feb. 1909	K-209
West, Elijah A., married	30 Aug. 1867	B-158
Weston, Arthur W., married	11 Dec. 1877	D-181
Weston, Henry L.; Caroline H.	20 Apr. 1861	A-346
Wetherbee, Nancy A.; Alva	12 Oct. 1866	B-25
Wetherbee, Retta, Mrs.; Fred B.	22 June 1909	K-236
Weyhe, Elizabeth; C. P.	16 Nov. 1889	F-625
Weyl, Ellenor, Mrs., married	4 Sep. 1868	B-261
Whaley, Rachel; Samuel	23 Apr. 1878	D-255
Whallone, Murray; Adelia Ann (B-554)	15 June 1867	B-120

Applicant and Family Information	Filing Date	Vol.-Pg.
Wharton, John Henry; no wife mentioned; 3 children	26 Jan. 1876	C-483
Wheaton, Alice J.; John T.	6 May 1904	J-13
Wheeler, Abbie E.; Edgar H.; 3 minors	20 Nov. 1916	L-313
Wheeler, Emma A.; Ira A., husband	8 Feb. 1916	L-253
Wheeler, Jacob F.; Martha M.	28 June 1905	J-80
Wheeler, Oliver; Ida M.	28 May 1915	L-180
Wheelock, Eliza, unmarried, head of family; children: Chas. R., Mary E., over 21 yrs., unable to care for themselves	5 Aug. 1891	G-215
Whelan, Michael widower	10 Apr. 1897	H-573
Whipple, I. C.	8 Dec. 1860	A-64
Whipple, K. H.; wife	25 Mar. 1893	G-404
Whipple, Lillian; John R.	24 May 1914	L-179
Whitaker, Elmira E.; G. N.	15 Nov. 1899	I-222
Whitaker, M. S.; wife	31 Jan. 1903	I-430
Whitaker, Mary E.; Walter L.	30 June 1908	K-136
Whitaker, Maude; Mark S.	19 Oct. 1920	M-53
White, Carie C.; E. J.	1 June 1881	E-97
White, Clara D.; John	24 May 1910	K-322
White, Edith Lewis; Edwin D.	18 Sep. 1917	L-369
White, Elijah F.; Margaret	20 Mar. 1862	A-410
White, Eliza J., married	12 Aug. 1873	C-199
White, Eliza Jane, widow over 77 yrs age; children: 7; living: Maria, Geo., Daniel (F-76)	25 Aug. 1904	J-27
White, Eliza L.; Geo. F.	28 Jan. 1897	H-526
White, I. M.; Florence H.	15 Sep. 1915	L-216
White, Mary Alice; John C.	18 Feb. 1901	I-317
White, Nancy C.; John M.	23 July 1872	C-117
Whiting, Charles; wife	3 Aug. 1905	J-89
Whitlock, May, widow of J. M.	9 July 1880	E-18
Whitman, Geo. W., head of family	10 May 1876	B-666
Whitman, Henry H., head of family	17 Sep. 1879	D-463
Whitman, Mary S., J. H.; probate	7 Jan. 1887	D-284
Whitmore, Charles A.; Laura M.; 4 minors	30 Apr. 1917	L-345
Whitney, Asahel; Harriet	15 Jan. 1868	B-184
Whittier, John F., married	11 Aug. 1876	D-35
Whitton, Jesse W.; Missouri A., wife	1 Apr. 1867	B-99
Wiander, Sofia; Emil; minor children	3 Apr. 1917	L-341
Wiatt, C. W.; Martha E.	7 June 1909	K-233
Wiatt, Lemarcus; Martha A.	5 May 1874	C-307

Applicant and Family Information	Filing Date	Vol.-Pg.
Widman, Adolph; Mary	22 May 1872	C-99
Wiedersham, Henry; Louisa Schwitzer	2 Aug. 1860	A-6
Wieling, Minnie; P.	4 Oct. 1909	K-268
Wier, Mary, widow; probate	27 Aug. 1869	B-44
Wiers, Margaret (probate book & page no. not listed on record)	8 May 1893	
Wiesenfeld, Herman; wife	3 Oct. 1904	J-36
Wiggin, Henry H., married	24 Apr. 1877	D-121
Wigton, Thomas; Marion; children Thomas, Jr.; Robert	31 Mar. 1919	L-465
Wilbert, John L.; Ardilla	20 June 1870	B-420
Wilde, Louis, married	23 Apr. 1872	C-85
Wilds, Mrs. D. T.; Barney	23 Jan. 1890	G-1
Wiley, Maude; James N.	30 Aug. 1888	F-500
Wiley, John; Lucy Ann	24 Apr. 1861	A-268
Wilfley, Roda A., married	15 Mar. 1871	B-507
Wilkerson, W. C.; wife	30 July 1884	E-491
Wilkins, Chas. P.; Emily C. nee Peterson; 3 children (10/13/1862, A-512) Maria Dallas, Henrietta, Wm.	26 Apr. 1862	A-479
Wilkins, Fannie L.; James S.	17 Sep. 1912	K-450
Wilkinson, Jeremiah; Eliza	2 June 1876	D-72
Wilkinson, Kate E.; Ollie T.	2 Nov. 1917	L-379
Wilks, Wm.; Elizabeth J. (5/4/1865, A-647)	7 Mar. 1864	A-592
Willey; J. M.; Mrs. Eliza M. (10/2/1889, E-586)	20 Aug. 1884	E-498
Williams, Alfred A. C., married	18 Jan. 1870	B-376
Williams, Allen; Barbara Ann	30 Mar. 1861	A-181
Williams, Celia S.; widow of Frank	16 Aug. 1892	G-336
Williams, Charles; Harriet F.	9 Aug. 1890	G-99
Williams, Charlotte; John (9/26/1883, E-380)	22 July 1879	D-437
Williams, Dora L.; V. M., dec'd, probate	11 Feb. 1888	D-399
Williams, E. P.; N. F., wife	21 Jan. 1882	E-181
Williams, Ellen M., widow; 1 minor dau.	16 Apr. 1914	L-163
Williams, Isaac S.; Elizabeth	4 Mar. 1861	A-197
Williams, J. G., married	17 Sep. 1874	C-328
Williams, James M.; Rachel S.	24 Sep. 1867	B-144
Williams, Jno. S.; Amanda M.	5 Oct. 1860	A-31
Williams, Lewis; Elizabeth	11 Jan. 1861	A-106
Williams, Maude E.; John H.	11 Sep. 1916	L-303
Williams, May E.; J. C., husband	16 Jan. 1919	L-454
Williams, Sarah E., head of family; unmarried sister Julia C. Fyfe and her minor child who Sarah supports; Sarah has	30 July 1895	H-247

Applicant and Family Information	Filing Date	Vol.-Pg.
husband		
Williams, Sarah F.; W. H.	21 Oct. 1887	F-422
Williams, William; wife	7 Dec. 1893	H-10
Williamson, S. E., Mrs.; husband	13 Oct. 1879	D-473
Williamson, Sarah A.; Henry	10 Jan. 1881	E-60
Willis, Abraham, married (11/17/1874, C-342)	6 Dec. 1872	B-611
Willits, Nancy A.; Wm. H. (12/30/1884, E-535)	27 Mar. 1883	E-318
Willson, Amelia; husband Charles	31 May 1864	A-610
Willson, H. M.; A. L.	28 Feb. 1861	A-133
Willson, H. M.; wife of J. C. (3/2/1886, F-235)	18 Feb. 1886	F-233
Wilscholt, Margaret; Theodore, dec'd	9 July 1891	F-633
Wilson, B. F.; Rebecca	29 Nov. 1879	D-494
Wilson, Bessie E.; Edwin A.	12 Oct. 1889	E-600
Wilson, E. A. (promiscuous records)	3 June 1903	G-65
Wilson, Edward Guy; Margaret Ann	25 Mar. 1879	D-391
Wilson, Edwin A.; Bessie E.	14 Feb. 1902	I-377
Wilson, Frederick; Bridget	2 May 1870	B-402
Wilson, James R., married	30 Mar. 1870	B-394
Wilson, John C. A.; Elizabeth A.	23 Apr. 1861	A-338
Wilson, Joseph S.; Eleanor A.	18 Feb. 1899	I-181
Wilson, Henderson; Mary (12/23/1875, C-471)	7 July 1869	B-339
Wilson, Laura; P. L., husband	27 Sep. 1916	L-274
Wilson, Mary E.; John G. (6/5/1862?)	7 Feb. 1862	A-490
Wilson, Myrtle; Henry F.	14 Apr. 1908	K-116
Wilson, Nellie B.; Ned S.	22 Dec. 1914	L-125
Wilson, Robt. D.	2 Mar. 1864	A-591
Wilson, Steve H.; Rosa	10 June 1908	K-129
Wilson, Susanna B., W. L., husband	18 Jan. 1862	A-397
Wilson, Sylvester H.; Rebecca	17 Apr. 1861	A-257
Wilson, Wm.; Louisa; 1 minor	17 Nov. 1871	C-5
Wilson, Wm. F.; Charlotte B.	27 Nov. 1900	I-282
Wilson, Wm. H.; Emma G. (4/24/1867, B-104)	3 Jan. 1867	B-63
Wilson, William H.; Isabella	27 June 1908	K-135
Wilson, William Percy; Sophia	29 June 1876	C-540
Wilsey, Cordelia; F.	27 Oct. 1860	A-48
Wilsey, R. G., unmarried	13 June 1898	I-86
Wilton, Thomas G., no family	1 Feb. 1894	H-20
Winchester, W. F.; Mary E.; Walter, age 3; Merlyn, age 15 mo.	22 Nov. 1915	L-233

Applicant and Family Information	Filing Date	Vol.-Pg.
Winder, Mary A.; Edward	30 July 1874	B-658
Winkler, Mrs. Carrie, widow of J.	17 July 1886	F-288
Winkler, Jacob, married	1 Feb. 1873	B-630
Winquist, Johanna; Peter	6 May 1882	E-213
Winter, Anne; T. P.	29 Mar. 1879	D-398
Winter, Annie; F. P.	28 Aug. 1883	E-371
Winterburn, John; wife	18 Oct. 1878	D-342
Winters, Chas. H.; wife	9 Jan. 1905	J-51
Winters, Dennis; Ellen	20 Nov. 1871	B-582
Winters, Lawrence	11 Oct. 1889	E-598
Wise, Elbert; Harriet A.	28 July 1873	C-206
Wise, Meyer; Berta	13 Apr. 1867	B-101
Wisecarver, Wm. H.; Mary	1 July 1873	C-180
Wiswell, Emily A.; J. A.	25 Jan. 1868	B-188
Witbro, Ole P.; Katrina	17 Feb. 1902	I-379
Witkinson, Lydia; Leander, dec'd; 3 minors	28 Mar. 1914	L-67
Witt, Charlotte, widow of Andrew S. (L.)	26 June 1876	C-538
Woerner, John; Josephine	24 Mar. 1909	K-216
Wolseth, Karen J.; Jens J.; 4 children	19 Aug. 1919	L-489
Wolverton, Charles E.; wife	15 Oct. 1896	H-492
Wood, Ben S., married (8/16/1888, F-491)	26 June 1883	E-347
Wood, John H.; wife	27 Nov. 1882	E-290
Wood, Joseph; wife	27 Oct. 1891	G-256
Wood, N. B.; Evaline	19 Apr. 1861	A-294
Wood, Oscar H.; wife	2 Jan. 1912	K-407
Wood, Wesley; wife	24 Feb. 1883	E-314
Wooden, Joseph; married	3 Feb. 1871	B-491
Woodruff, Catherine, was married	28 Oct. 1878	D-346
Woods, J. D., married	7 Mar. 1870	B-384
Woods, James	22 Apr. 1861	A-262
Woods, Mrs. Margaret; John	14 Dec. 1897	I-25
Woods, Mary A.; Wm. M.	18 Dec. 1873	C-267
Woodward, Chas. W., married	1 Dec. 1873	C-261
Woodward, Mrs. M. J.; C. W.	14 Jan. 1884	E-420
Woodward, Martha Jane, widow of Orrin	3 May 1907	K-42
Woodworth, Cynthia B.; S. C.	29 Feb. 1872	C-52
Woodworth, Jannette E.; Scott J.	13 May 1875	C-397
Woodworth, L. M.; E. C., husband	10 Sep. 1918	L-429

Applicant and Family Information	Filing Date	Vol.-Pg.
Woodworth, Scott J.; married	25 May 1870	B-407
Wooldridge, Elizabeth; Edmund	25 Apr. 1861	A-360
Wooley, William S.; Margaret	24 Mar. 1868	B-214
Woolsey, Martha A.; Ezra W.	2 June 1883	E-341
Woolsey, Charles F.; Mrs. Nellie C.; 8 children	11 Aug. 1914	L-96
Wooster, Mark, married	25 Mar. 1865	A-644
Wormell, L. J., married	7 Dec. 1874	C-349
Worth, Lewis W.; Elizabeth M. (3/19/1861, A-167)	27 Oct. 1860	A-42
Worthmann, Rebecca; C. H.	8 July 1908	K-142
Wratten, G. L.; Emilie M. (8/23/1867, C-593; 4/23/1861, A-251; 2/6/1863, A-537)	2 Jan. 1866	A-687
Wright, B. C., married	11 Oct. 1866	B-32
Wright, Blanche E.; Sampson B.	12 May 1890	G-39
Wright, Fannie L.; Sampson B.	6 Apr. 1885	F-44
Wright, Francis C.; Catherine (10/5/1907, K-78)	17 Apr. 1879	D-402
Wright, H. J.; Harriet F.	16 Mar. 1911	K-372
Wright, Isaac, married; 1 grandchild (5/12/1873, C-135; 10/17/1904, J-39)	2 Mar. 1877	D-96
Wright, John E., married	3 Sep. 1877	D-140
Wright, Joseph; wife	17 Apr. 1880	D-555
Wright, Kate; E. L.	2 June 1902	I-393
Wright, Loretta; Benjamin C.	19 May 1920	M-33
Wright, Lucinda; Isaac (5/27/1903, I-453)	8 July 1890	G-75
Wright, Mary A.; Chas. B.	12 Nov. 1900	I-303
Wright, Nancy Jane; John E.	5 Aug. 1874	C-321
Wyatt, Lemarcus; Martha Ann (12/10/1864)	4 Jan. 1865	A-633
Wyatt, Martha A., Mrs.; Lemarcus	8 Sep. 1862	A-503
Wyckoff, Amos A.; wife	25 May 1899	I-206
Wyckoff, Elizabeth, married	6 Sep. 1866	B-40
Wyckoff, Henry, married	14 Aug. 1866	A-708
Wycoff, G. H.; wife	4 Jan. 1879	D-372
Wyland, S. I.; Nellie H.; 1 child	8 Dec. 1915	L-239
Wyrick, Mary A.; H. R.	29 Jan. 1901	I-315

Applicant and Family Information	Filing Date	Vol.-Pg.
Yandle, Mrs. Catherine; Frederick J.	14 June 1890	G-53
Yates, Hannah T.; John W.; probate	19 May 1896	F-426
Yates, Owen C.; wife	13 June 1889	F-583
Yates, T. M., unmarried	4 May 1895	H-217
Yeager, Annie; J. E.	5 Nov. 1906	K-13
Yeager, Lizzie; J. D.	17 Jan. 1902	I-373
Yeagley. Henry; Sidney, wife	29 July 1881	E-120
Youle, Adam W., widower; family	8 Mar. 1868	B-208
Young, Bridget (promiscuous records)	7 Jan. 1903	
Young, Carrie B.; Dr. Byrd, dec'd (11/28/1892, E-427, probate)	4 Feb. 1891	G-164
Young, D. C.; Mariah E.	8 Jan. 1872	C-28
Young, Ernest L.; Loula Farr Young, wife; 3 children	27 May 1919	L-476
Young, Eva Della; Clarence H.	26 Mar. 1918	L-403
Young, Frank W.; wife	30 Oct. 1878	D-349
Young, James B.; Olivia	15 Nov. 1860	A-50
Young, Jennie; A. H.	26 Feb. 1881	E-78
Young, Jennie; D. E.	12 Dec. 1901	I-370
Young, John, married	4 June 1868	B-239
Young, John; R. S., wife	26 July 1901	I-345
Young, Mary L.; J. B.	24 Aug. 1888	F-496
Young, Michael, married	5 Nov. 1873	C-253
Young, Sarah A.; John S.	3 Aug. 1895	H-251
Young, James B.; Olivia	15 Nov. 1860	A-50
Young, Jennie; A. H.	26 Feb. 1881	E-78

Applicant and Family Information	Filing Date	Vol.-Pg.
Zandrino, Gaspero; 3 yr. old dau. Giuseppino; mother Giuseppino	17 Feb. 1904	I-948
Zandrino, Giusepino; Stephens	4 Nov. 1891	G-265
Zane, Mrs. Jane; A. J.	4 June 1885	F-64
Zane, M. A.; wife of J. M.	14 May 1887	F-390
Zartman, Wm.; Rhoda	16 Apr. 1861	A-222
Zech, Sarah W.; Wm.	24 Oct. 1919	M-7
Zeb, H.; Anna; 1 child H. P., age 8 yrs.	8 Feb. 1904	I-496
Zeller, Bertha; John	19 Sep. 1882	E-264
Zimmerman, Mattie E.; J. R.	27 Sep. 1920	M-52
Zimmerman, Ruby; Paul	25 June 1917	L-356
Zimmermann, Mary C.; F. E.	14 Jan. 1904	I-490
Zink, Otto; Eugenie	25 Jan. 1906	J-119
Zoeller, Henry; Marzella, wife	24 Feb. 1871	B-503
Zunino, Maria; Lorenzo, husband	1 Apr. 1915	L-158
Zurcher, Martha L.; Ulysses, husband	13 Sep. 1915	L-215
Zurlo, Teresa; Domenik, husband	22 June 1915	L-187
Zuur, Louisa; John	14 Mar. 1914	L-66

Other Heritage Books by the Sonoma County Genealogical Society, Inc.:

CD: *Sonoma County [California] Records, Volume 1*

Early School Attendance Records of Sonoma County, California, Beginning 1858

Early School Attendance Records of Sonoma County, California, Volume II: 1874–1932

Homestead Declarations: Amended Index, Sonoma County, California, Second Edition

Index and Abstracts of Wills, Sonoma County, California: 1850–1900

Index to Naturalization Records in Sonoma County, California, Volume 1: 1841–1906

Naturalization Records in Sonoma County, California, Volume II: 1906–1930

Index to The Sonoma Searcher*: Volume 16, No. 1 to Volume 28, No. 3*
(Including Index to The Sonoma Searcher*: Volume 1, No. 1 to Volume 15, No. 4, SCGS, August 1993)*

Index to Vital Data in Local Newspapers of Sonoma County, California, Volume 1: 1855–1875

Index to Vital Data in Local Newspapers of Sonoma County, California, Volume 2: 1876–1880

Index to Vital Data in Local Newspapers of Sonoma County, California, Volume 3: 1881–1885

Index to Vital Data in Local Newspapers of Sonoma County, California, Volume 4: 1886–1890

Index to Vital Data in Local Newspapers of Sonoma County, California, Volume 5: 1891–1899

Index to Vital Data in Local Newspapers of Sonoma County, California, Volume 6: 1900–1903

Index to Vital Data in Local Newspapers of Sonoma County, California, Volume 7: 1904–1906

Index to Vital Data in Local Newspapers of Sonoma County, California, Volume 8: 1907–1909

Index to Vital Data in Local Newspapers of Sonoma County, California, Volume 9: 1910–1912

Indigent Records in Sonoma County, California 1878 to 1926, Volume 1: The Indigents

Indigent Records in Sonoma County, California 1878 to 1926, Volume 2: Taxpayers Who Certified Indigent Need

Militia Lists of Sonoma County, California, 1846 to 1900

Santa Rosa Rural Cemetery, 1853–1997

Sonoma County, California Cemetery Records, 1846–1921, Third Edition

Sonoma County, California Death Records, 1873–1905, Second Edition

Sonoma County California Reconstructed 1890 Census

The 1930 School Census of Sonoma County, California

www.ingramcontent.com/pod-product-compliance
Lightning Source LLC
Chambersburg PA
CBHW080336270326
41927CB00014B/3251